ENJOYING THE HUMBERHEAD LEVELS

Dedicated to the many people who, in their different ways,
have contributed to the value and future of the
Humberhead Levels and Moors.

Enjoying the
HUMBERHEAD LEVELS

Roly Smith

HALSGROVE

First published in 2004 by Halsgrove
Text © 2004 Roly Smith
Photographs © 2004 Peter and Janet Roworth, unless otherwise stated

Cover illustrations: Front (main): *An aerial view of a flooded Thorne Moors in 1997, showing old peat workings*
Inset l-r: *Four-wheel drive tractor on warpland; Large heath butterflies; The Festival of the Plough, Epworth*
Back: *Drax Power Station, seen from the edge of the Yorkshire Wolds*

ISBN 1 84114 399 5

British Library Cataloguing-in-Publication-Data
A CIP data record for this book is available from the British Library

HALSGROVE
Halsgrove House
Lower Moor Way
Tiverton EX16 6SS
T: 01884 243242
F: 01884 243325
www.halsgrove.com

Printed and bound by D'Auria Industrie Grafiche Spa, Italy

Foreword

By Roy Clarke, Chairman of the Burnet Trust

'Enjoying the Humberside Levels.' Does that sound like fun to you? In the first place where is it? And if it's so level, what's to enjoy?

Well, this book will tell you.

There are people who will not accept that natural beauty in scenery is possible without a mountain in it or at least a few hills. They might easily pass us by, here on our levels, on their way to find something worth looking at. The view through a windscreen misses our big sky.

There was a time, quite recently, when it seemed that our native landscape was doomed to disappear and that all we'd have left to lift our spirits would be that big sky. This book will tell you about the processes which were leading to that dismal prospect and about the people and events responsible for their reversal – responsible, in fact, for the optimism which is now thankfully in place.

I live in this area. I love my bit of it but I have to confess to feeling ashamed at how little I really knew about it compared to the author of this book. Roly Smith gives us an astonishing amount of information. The pages are laden with fact but never leaden. There are two ways to present a mass of information. One – and by far the more usual – is to be very boring. The second is to be informative and at the same time lively, anecdotal and entertaining. I promise you that the first thing you will enjoy about 'Enjoying the Humberside Levels' is the book itself.

Roy Clarke
Sykehouse
September 2004

Acknowledgements

Flood waters of the Derwent approach Aughton church

The author wishes to extend his grateful thanks, among others he may have forgotten, to Stuart Pasley, Countryside Agency (whose idea the book was); my good friend Ian Carstairs (for his photography and support throughout); Peter and Janet Roworth (for their excellent photography); Simon Warner; Roy Clarke for his foreword; Colin Howes and Martin Limbert at the Doncaster Museum and Art Gallery; Mr Pye at the Howden Bookshop; Tim Kohler, English Nature (for the day out on Thorne Moors); Martin Moss, Countryside Agency (especially for his Pilgrim Fathers lead); Keith Miller of English Heritage; Margaret Price, Epworth Tourism Partnership; Julian Rollins; Ian Rotherham, Sheffield Hallam University; Joanna Royle, Yorkshire Tourist Board, and Peter Skidmore.

Contents

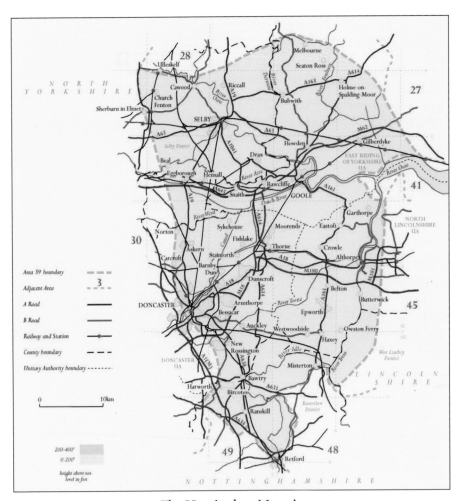

The Humberhead Levels

I. Introduction

Any fool can appreciate mountain scenery,
but it takes a man of discernment to appreciate the fens

A fenman quoted in Catherine Caufield's
Thorne Moors (1991)

You won't find the Humberhead Levels marked on any map. The name is an invention coined by the seminal national study of the character of the English landscape published in 1998.

If you look on any standard road map, the area between the A161 Gainsborough to Goole road and the M18 motorway is one of the largest areas in England which is completely blank. Few roads cross it and the villages are few and far between.

The lozenge-shaped area extends over about 880 square miles (2275 sq km) and roughly speaking covers the low-lying region between the Vale of York beyond the Ouse to the north, to the Vales of the Trent and Belvoir in the south. The western boundary is the southern Magnesian limestone ridge, and the eastern, the first slopes of the Yorkshire Wolds in the north and Lincolnshire Edge to the south.

It covers parts of three counties – Yorkshire, North Lincolnshire and Nottinghamshire – and several contrasting landscape types. These range from the virtual wilderness of Thorne and Hatfield Moors – the largest area of lowland raised bog in England and an internationally-important wildlife site – to some of the most fertile and productive arable areas in the country.

So within minutes you can be transported from the boggy, peat-dominated expanses of Thorne Moors to the enormous, geometric, prairie-like fields of the areas around Crowle, Epworth and Wroot. Many people have compared this area with the Somerset Levels, the Fens of East Anglia, or perhaps more accurately in view of its history, the reclaimed polderlands of the Netherlands. It comes as no surprise to learn that the area around Thorne was once dubbed 'Little Holland.'

Travelling across it on a bright late spring day, you marvel at the way the hedgeless roads suddenly and for no reason go into a series of sharp Z bends, when there is no apparent obstacle in sight. The only occasional relief is a blowsy avenue of white-candled horse chestnuts – a popular tree on the Levels – or billowing white-blossomed hawthorn belts around isolated, pantile-roofed villages.

The view from the highest point – the hillfort-topped 269ft/82m Gringley Beacon on the southern edge of the Levels – extends northwards for 40 miles to the distant Gothic towers of York Minster across a flat, chequerboard-covered tableland of rich farming country, highlighted by the splashes of vivid mustard yellow of oilseed rape or the rich green of young corn.

One common characteristic is the enormous, over-arching skies, where you can see the weather coming long before it hits you, and where your view of the horizon is usually uncluttered by hills, buildings, or even trees. Often the only landmarks in the far distance are the steaming cauldrons of the Trent and Aire Valley power stations, such as Drax, Eggborough or Ferrybridge, adding their own plumes of man-made cumulus to the sky, the marching electricity pylons, the occasional church spire or truncated former windmill.

Catherine Caufield wrote of Thorne and Hatfield Moors: "In these unprettied places, one feels entirely free of the works of man. They impart feelings of desolation, of emptiness, of peace."

To find some kind of unity in the varied landscapes of the Humberhead Levels we must go back 14,000 years to the end of the last Ice Age, when virtually the

Looking north across the Humberhead Levels from Gringley on the Hill

whole of the area was under the shallow waters of the great glacial Lake Humber. The Escrick moraine left by the glacier to the south of York marked the northern boundary of that huge lake which flooded the land as far south as Misterton and Doncaster, leaving only islands of slightly higher ground at places like the Isle of Axholme, Hatfield, Crowle and Snaith. It was the level sediments left by Lake Humber which were to lay the foundations of the essential flatness of the modern landscape and the clay subsoil which still exists beneath later deposits.

Five thousand years ago, during the Neolithic period, most of the Humberhead Levels were covered,

Road, drain and arable land near Wroot

Typical Humberhead farming landscape, near Crowle

as was the rest of Britain, by the wildwood – an impenetrable forest of broadleaved trees, such as lime, oak, hazel and ash. Some of these trees, thousands of years old, are still emerging from the peat bogs of Thorne and Hatfield, uncovered by erosion, deep ploughing and the extensive commercial peat diggings which have transformed and industrialised the landscape.

The deep layer of peat which covers about half of the area is the result of the prehistoric clearance of woodland and the introduction of waterlogged conditions about 4,000 years ago. The nutrient-poor, acidic conditions in the resulting huge swampy marshland, were perfect for the formation of peat-forming mosses like the bright, lime-green sphagnum. When the mosses died, they could not decay in this waterlogged, airless and bacteria-free environment, but built up in layer upon layer of dead organic material – which eventually became the rich brown peat so much in demand by gardeners.

Gradually over the years the peat built up to a depth of around 20 feet/6 m, and it formed one of the largest and most impenetrable wildernesses in lowland Britain. Local people had always taken small amounts of the peat from the edges for fuel, and the marshes were used for traditional pursuits such as wild-fowling and hunting, but there was nothing like the large-scale devastation which followed the commercial extraction of peat which began about a century ago. Nearly 3,500 acres (1,381ha) of the area is now protected as the Humberhead Peatlands National Nature Reserve (NNR) and commercial peat extraction has now ended on Thorne Moors and is shortly to end at Hatfield.

The other extractive industry which has left an indelible mark on the landscape of the Humberhead Levels is coal mining. By the end of the 1960s, more than 50 collieries in the South Yorkshire coalfield were

A former windmill: Maw's Mill, near Epworth

producing 30 per cent of the country's coal output. It was a vital part of the local economy of the villages in the western part of the Humberhead Levels. Today, however, most of the old pits have closed down, and their sites have been reclaimed.

Thorne Moors

The modern landscape of the Humberhead Levels is dominated by large-scale, intensive agriculture which utilises some of the richest and most productive farmland in England. It is a landscape which essentially was brought about by some of the earliest land reclamation schemes in the country, engineered by Dutch and French 'participants' led by Cornelius Vermuyden during the seventeenth century.

Local people had always realised the fertility created by the winter flooding of their fields, but the Dutchmen changed the landscape in a far more permanent, some would say damaging, way (for Vermuyden's work was not a success) by actually changing the courses of rivers in an attempt to drain the marshland and bring it into cultivation. Later, the Water Authorities (now the water companies), the National Rivers Authority and the Internal Drainage Boards (IDBs), which are now responsible for arterial drainage, had a long and distinguished history in protecting lives from flooding and the efficient drainage of land for agriculture on the Levels.

What is left today is a prairie landscape which can remind the visitor of the great cornfields of Canada and the mid-Western USA. "Rust-red pantiled barns, sometimes showing Dutch influence, stand moored in what seems like a boundless sea of wheat and barley," wrote Jeremy Purseglove in *Taming the Flood*. "There is a sense of infinite space and silence, as if the rippling oceans of grain are just an extension of the huge emptiness of the North Sea, whose waves beat against the shore, actually above the level of this land, a few miles to the north-east."

But the 150 or so miles of ruler-straight dykes which criss-cross this productive land in an intricate web of drainage channels running into the Trent, the Ouse and then the Humber leave you in no doubt that this is still a wetland at heart.

There seems to be something in wetlands like the Humberhead Levels that breeds rebels. As a early nineteenth century writer observed: "So wild a country nurses up a race of people as wild." Vermuyden and his Participants were fiercely opposed by the Humberhead fenmen, and there were riots when they realised that their ancient rights and way of life were threatened. Even today, nearly four centuries later, local people still speak of the coming of 'the Dutchmen' with a level of resentment. William Bradford, one of the Pilgrim Fathers who first settled in North America in 1620, hailed from Austerfield, and the area later became a stronghold of the Parliamentarian cause when the Civil War broke out in 1642, and has long had a very strong tradition of independent freeholders.

So it may be no coincidence then that Epworth on the Isle of Axholme was the birthplace of Methodism and the home of John Wesley, whose fiery brand of evangelism was to sweep across the world. Today, pilgrims from a Methodist congregation estimated at 70 million all over the globe come to visit the beautiful red brick Queen Anne rectory which was his home. They also visit the parish church of St Andrew's where, when he was barred from the building, Wesley famously preached from the top of his father's tomb in the churchyard.

A new spirit of evangelism and the prospect of a bright new future is sweeping across the Humberhead Levels today. The message is now one of sustainable development, epitomised by the 'Value in Wetness' initiative, which looks at how to make water and land management more sustainable for the future, and which has received the support of many farmers and landowners. It could provide a blueprint and influence

Unused headgear, recently demolished, at the former Thorne Colliery

future wetland policies not only here in Britain but throughout Europe.

After years of neglect, the future now being faced by the communities of the Humberhead Levels is an exciting one as considerable efforts are made by many people and agencies to save, maintain and enhance this unique landscape.

These include the Green Tourism Forum, which is developing sustainable recreational opportunities in the area, such as the Peatland Way long distance footpath, and local community regeneration projects such as Selby's Leader+, the North Doncaster Development Trust, and the Thorne Market Town Initiative. Local charitable trusts such as the Burnet Trust and the Carstairs Countryside Trust are working with local communities to save and manage valuable sites such as Sutton Common, and local food sourcing is being promoted by groups such as the Doncaster Local Food Network.

All these projects are aiming to rejuvenate the social, economic and environmental well-being of local communities and creating a bright, new and exciting future for the Levels. The recent development of the former RAF airbase at Finningley as the 'Robin Hood Doncaster Sheffield' international airport is seen as another potential catalyst for the economic regeneration of the area.

But as the historical significance and subtle attractiveness of the vast and varied landscapes of the Humberhead Levels come to be appreciated more fully, visitors will hopefully still be able to discern that sense of "infinite space and silence" which is so rare in today's hectic world.

VALUE IN WETNESS

The five key objectives in the Value in Wetness Initiative are:-
• Integrated economic, social and environmental aims for sustainable water and land management in arable areas
• Proof that alternative management of water could bring environmental, social and economic benefits
• Practical methods of achieving the objectives, including small site demonstrations, and practical ways of implementing the EU Water Frameworks Directive
• Recommendations concerning the changes required to other policies to assist and add value to implementation of the Directive
• Analysis of the potential for the Internal Drainage Boards to have a broader and more positive role in water management

A HUMBERHEAD GLOSSARY

Bog oak – ancient trees preserved under the peat
Brier-berries – blackberries
Cleat boards – type of broad wooden 'skis' used by marshmen to cross boggy areas
Decoy – funnel-like traps for catching ducks
Drain – an artifical drainage channel
Dyke – another name for an artifical drainage channel
Gale – local name for bog myrtle
Gofer – a cake made from batter (from the Dutch *gaufres*)
Graving – the cutting of peat
Gyme – large pond scoured out by flood water when a river breaks its banks
Hetherd – old dialect name for the adder
Little Men of Wroot – local name for midges
Moor buzzard – hen harrier
Moldiwarp – a mole
Participants – mainly Dutch and French businessmen who backed Vermuyden's drainage scheme
Piper – a dog trained to tempt ducks into decoys
Sewer – yet another name for a drainage channel
Silk grass – cotton grass
Snickle – an animal trap
Stilts – also used by marshmen to cross boggy areas
Trying – probing for bog timber
Turbary – the commoners' right to cut turf or peat
Warping – deliberate enriching of land with river silts either by seasonal flooding or introduced soil

2. The West

It's hard to believe that the former coal mining town of Askern on the A19 north of Doncaster was once a health spa to rival Harrogate, Buxton and Bath. Apart from its pleasant lake in the centre of the village, Askern seems at first sight to be typical of many in the former South Yorkshire coalfield.

The restored waste tips of the former pit at the northern end are beginning to be assimilated back into the landscape, but the rows of terraced miners' cottages remain, and social life still centres around the Miners' Welfare Hall.

But before the opening of the colliery in 1911, Askern had been a popular Victorian spa town, attracting visitors who arrived on direct daily trains from as far away as Liverpool, Bradford and Manchester, and even further afield.

The waters of Askern had been first mentioned as early as 1734 by Dr. Short of Sheffield in his book *Mineral Waters of Yorkshire*. The then lord of the Manor, Viscount Galway, and Humphrey Osbaldeston erected a stone building in 1794 over the site of the spa.

But it was the 1820s which saw the real development of the total of five wells, offering their curative properties to visitors. The waters of the Askern springs were reputed to be beneficial in curing diseases ranging from rheumatism, gout and indigestion to various skin complaints.

A contemporary guidebook boasted of the beautiful surrounding scenery and the dry, bracing air, and claimed "an unequalled climate and the best sulphur springs in England". Carriage rides were popular around the local villages and there even was a "Lovers' Walk" at the rear of the Pool. To serve the visitors, there were a total of six hotels, and over forty boarding houses in Askern had rooms which were let out for the season. It was said that on a Bank Holiday, the population of Askern could treble.

The largest bathhouse was the 90-room Spa Hydropathic Establishment, which stood on a three-acre site overlooking the lake, by the side of what is now the A19 where the Alexander House community building stands today. The Hydro contained dancing, recreation, dining, drawing, billiard, smoking, reading and writing rooms – and even boasted its own doctor and a 'lady entertainer'!

Askern's lake is still one of the most attractive features of the town, and it too played an important part in the development of the spa. In Victorian times it was known as The Pool, and was described in a guidebook of the time as "giving to the whole village a seaside appeal."

In more recent times, Askern has been in the headlines for the archaeological work which has been carried out by Sheffield, Hull and Exeter Universities on a site to the south of the village at Sutton Common. Two prehistoric enclosures have been excavated and have been described as a 'marsh fort' and dated to the Iron Age – around 350 BC.

An early nineteenth century engraving of the Manor Baths at Askern

A unique partnership project headed by the Carstairs Countryside Trust – the owners of the common – and various local and national bodies and the local community, has saved the site from drying out and thus destroying the existing underground archaeological remains, by a process known as 're-wetting.'

The castles at nearby Conisbrough and Tickhill show that the areas to the south and west of the Levels were strategically important from Norman times onwards. Conisbrough in particular was the principal northern stronghold of the de Warenne family, Earls of

Askern Pool

Surrey, between 1069 and 1347. The magnificent circular buttressed keep built by Hamelin Plantagenet in 1180, still lords it on its limestone ridge above the village, and is reckoned to be one of the finest examples of medieval castle architecture in Europe. It is now managed by the local Ivanhoe Trust by local agreement with English Heritage. The parish church of St Peter at Conisbrough is one of the oldest and most interesting in the area. Originally a Saxon minster dating from around 640, it still retains much Saxon work and has Norman and twelfth century aisles. The memorial chapel contains the original altar stone from the castle chapel.

Tickhill Castle is an altogether less well-preserved motte and bailey castle, part of the Duchy of Lancaster estate and not open to the public. It is thought to have been built around a partly-natural hill ('Tica's hill') on which a ten-sided stone shell keep was erected in the late eleventh century by the Norman baron Roger de Busli. Later it boasted a stone curtain wall and massive gatehouse, much of which still survives, despite some damage during the late 1640s at the end of the Civil War.

By far the largest settlement on the western side of the Humberhead Levels is the town of Doncaster, which is perhaps best-known for hosting in September the oldest of the racing calendar's classics – the St Leger– on its famous racecourse.

Doncaster – 'the fort on the River Don' – was founded by the Romans who knew it as *Danum*. The town was granted its market charter in 1248, and it continues to this day featuring over 600 stalls in the great Victorian Market Hall, dating from the days when Doncaster was a major railway town. There are some fine Georgian buildings from the town's earlier heyday as racing and marketing centre, including the

St George's Church, Doncaster

Mansion House, designed by Paine, which is still the official home of the town's mayor, and one of only three in England. Dominating the town's skyline is the stately tower of St George's Parish Church, designed by George Gilbert Scott, the architect of St Pancras Station. The new Frenchgate shopping centre has a range of the regular High Street stores and designer boutiques.

Bawtry, on the River Idle to the south of Doncaster,

Frenchgate Centre, Doncaster

A former coaching inn; the Crown Hotel, Bawtry Market Place

The Mansion House, Doncaster: one of only three in England

was once an important inland entrepot port for the export of millstones quarried in the Peak District, as well as for knives and blades made in Sheffield and Rotherham. In essence, it is a planned town laid out at the end of the twelfth century to take advantage of the trade brought by the River Idle, although earlier activity is indicated by a Roman fortlet on the east bank of the Idle. The main Roman road to Doncaster, York and the north of England passed by here – the forerunner to the Great North Road. Later, Bawtry was to benefit from its proximity to the Great North Road turnpike. Interesting buildings include the medieval parish church of St Nicholas, the late seventeenth century gabled Dutch House in Church Street, and The Crown, a former coaching inn, in the High Street.

The tiny linear village of Austerfield, north of

Bawtry, was the home of William Bradford, one of the leaders of the Pilgrim Fathers, who traditionally is thought to have been born at Austerfield Manor House, the son of a yeoman farmer, in 1589 or 90. He became associated with the Separatist church at nearby Scooby and fled to Holland in 1607, returning to England to join the *Mayflower* pilgrims in 1620. Bradford went on to become the long-serving Governor and historian of Plymouth County in what is now Massachusetts, in New England (see box).

PILGRIM'S PROGRESS

A bronze statue on Plymouth waterfront in Massachusetts, New England, commemorates an Austerfield man who is remembered as perhaps the greatest of the Pilgrim Fathers. William Bradford, the son of a yeoman farmer, became involved with the Separatist church at nearby Scrooby and eventually fled to Holland in 1607. He returned to England in 1620 to join the pilgrims on the *Mayflower* on its two-month voyage across the Atlantic to America. Bradford went on to become Governor of the 'Plimoth Plantation' for 31 years and was the historian of the pioneering colony in what is now Massachusetts. His account of life in the colony, *Of Plymouth Plantation (1620-1647)* is the fullest account of the community. When Bradford died in 1657, he left an estate worth £900, including a 300-acre/741ha farm on the Jones River and a house at Plymouth set within an extensive garden and a library of almost 300 books.

COME FLY WITH ROBIN HOOD

The former RAF base at Finningley, to the south-east of Doncaster, is currently being redeveloped as a new £80 million international airport, with the unlikely name of 'Robin Hood Doncaster Sheffield Airport'. The naming was a brilliant publicity stroke which sparked worldwide debate and controversy. It was chosen by the developers, Peel Airports, because of the traditional association of the legendary medieval outlaw with this part of Yorkshire, and it predictably provoked a storm of protest from neighbouring Nottinghamshire. The airport will host flights to many parts of Europe and the 900-acre (365ha) site will also include an extensive business park, which has been heralded as a major tool in the economic regeneration of the region.

KILL OR CURE...

Askern's Pool was fed by several springs of both fresh and sulphur water and contained "profound pits, the depth whereof was not known." The spa sulphur water from the Pool was green in colour, and apparently rather unpalatable to drink. It was usually warmed for bathing, but was also drunk cold "with rhubarb and magnesia".

The strong sulphurous odour emitted from the waters caused one Victorian physician, Dr Edward Chorley, to pen the following doggerel poem:

The devil when passing Askeron
Was asked what he thought thereon:
Quoth Satan -'Judging from the stink
I can't be far from home, I think'.

3. Thorne and Hatfield Moors

The first known representation of Thorne and Hatfield Moors is on the so-called Inclesmoor Map held in London's Public Records Office. The map is thought to have been drawn sometime between 1410 and 1420, but Martin Taylor in *Thorne Mere & The Old River Don* thinks it could be connected with an enquiry into the rights of turbary (peat cutting) dating as far back as 1320.

It shows the area south of the Humber ('Humbre') to the Don ('Doen') as a bright green oasis threaded by rivers and decorated with representations of flowers and plants. It is difficult to pick out the names of places in the dense Latin Gothic lettering, but you can just about make out Hatfield ('Hatfeld') and Thorne ('Thourne'), and a great swirling whirlpool of water in the Don named 'Brathmer,' which appears to be the fabled Great Mere of Thorne.

This is where the last recorded hunt on the royal hunting preserve of Hatfield Chase took place in 1609, as shown in the famous contemporary painting of Thorne Mere. According to Abraham de la Pryme, vicar of Thorne in the early eighteenth century, the 15-year-old Prince Henry, James I's elder son and brother of Charles I, invited 'a Dutch engineer' believed to be Cornelius Vermuyden to a hunting party on the chase. Whatever the truth, the engineer may well have taken the opportunity to reconnoitre the prospects for drainage.

After rounding up about 500 deer, the hunting party drove them towards Thorne Mere, where nearly 100 boats were waiting. The deer took to the water and, according to Pryme, "this royal navy" of hunters swiftly embarked in pursuit onto the lake.

… there (the deer) being up to their necks in water their horned heads raised seemed to represent a little wood…

The scene was memorably depicted in the painting by an unknown artist, where Thorne Mere is shown under a stormy sky and the antlers of the trapped deer do indeed look like 'a little wood' in the middle of the lake.

Hatfield Chase (or Chace) was the largest unenclosed royal hunting deer park in England, extending over 180,000 acres/72,850ha. It included much of what is now Thorne and Hatfield Moors, and about half of the area was either mere or marshland. From 1460, it was subject to forest laws which forbade anyone other than the nobility to hunt there, but apparently, in the absence of a lord of the manor, the laws were not strictly enforced.

The Chase was governed by the King's Bow Bearer, later known as the Surveyor General. Under him were the Master or Chief Forester; five Keepers and 25 Regarders, who controlled the boundaries of the forest. The population of red and fallow deer was never large and there were very few large hunts like the 1609 event, although during one in 1541, 200 stags and does were killed in a single day.

When the Chase was 'disparked' in 1629, the moors

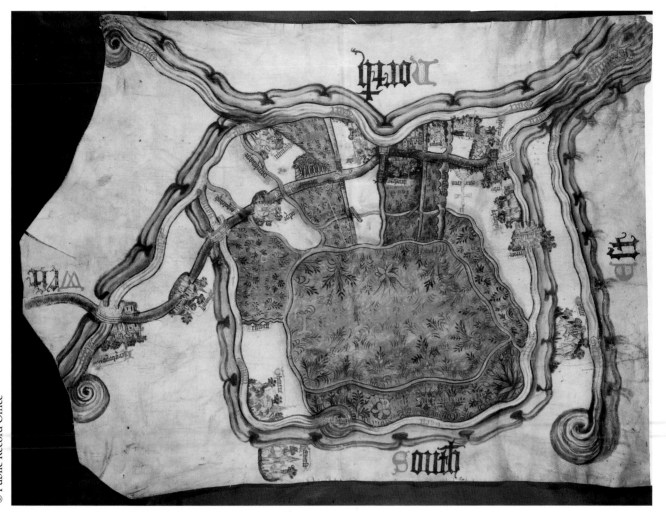

The Inclesmoor Map of Humberhead c.1450

reverted to their old, traditional use. Local people had used the common land of the moors for centuries for wildfowling, the cutting of turves of peat for fuel by exercising their right of turbary, and the finding and using of 'bog oaks.'

William Dugdale, writing the history of embanking, and the draining of rivers and fens in 1662, remarked on the discovery of these sunken timbers:

….great numbers of Oak, Firr, and other Trees, which have been of late frequently found in the Moor, upon making

Sunset over Thorne Moors, showing the silhouette of the former Thorne Colliery headgear, since demolished

of sundry Ditches and Chanels for the drayning thereof… Of which sort (oaks) there are multitudes, and of an extraordinary bignesse;

The black-stained timbers were so well preserved that there was a thriving trade in first finding them, by the use of iron rods (a process known as 'trying'), and then shaping them for uses as diverse as ships' keels and masts, fence palings and rails, ceiling laths, roofing timbers, gateposts or for fuel. The preservative properties of the peat meant that the timbers used for boats or fencing did not need painting or other preservatives.

But it is the commercial extraction of peat, as opposed to the small-scale hand-cutting for local use for fuel in the past, which has so damaged the ancient moorland wastes of Thorne and Hatfield in recent years. The Thorne Moors Improvement Company was formed in 1848 to drain the moors and convert them to farmland. Later, the British Moss Litter Company extracted peat commercially, initially for animal

Snow on old peat cuttings, Thorne Moors

Peat extraction on Hatfield Moors

bedding and later to be sold as garden compost. Peat extraction became fully mechanised in 1963 when Fisons acquired the company and embarked on large-scale drainage and excavation by huge machines, In 1987, Fisons introduced surface milling, which stripped the surface clear of vegetation before gradually ripping off layers of peat.

A long campaign by conservationists led by William Bunting of Thorne (see Chapter 6) which involved some direct action by his band of "Bunting's Beavers" eventually received backing of the Government, and will lead to the eventual cessation of commercial peat digging. Work on Thorne Moors has already stopped and cessation is imminent on Hatfield Moors. Two smaller workings still remain, one near Hatfield and on Crowle Moor, which is currently, as this book goes to press, the subject of a public enquiry.

Thorne Moors had been created a Site of Special Scientific Interest (SSSI) in 1970 and it later became part of the Humberhead Peatlands National Nature Reserve together with Hatfield Moors and parts of Crowle and Goole Moors. It is now the largest and most important lowland raised bog in England and its wildlife interest is recognised as a major driver for the economic rejuvenation of the area. Pioneering work is now underway by English Nature to "re-wet" the old peat workings, to give nature a helping hand in eventually restoring them to their former glory.

Coal mining has been the other great industry which has left an indelible mark on the landscape. The first colliery in the area opened at Conisbrough in 1894, and pits in the South Yorkshire coalfield gradually spread east after that. By the end of the 1960s, there were estimated to be 50,000 miners employed in more than 50 collieries in the coalfield, producing about 30 per cent of the country's output.

There were pits at Thorne, Bentley, Rossington, and Stainforth, and mining was a vital part of the local economy of the villages in this part of the Humberhead Levels up until the creation of the Selby coalfield in the 1970s. Today, however, there are no working collieries left and many of the old pit sites have been reclaimed. The skeletal twin towers of the winding gear of the former Thorne Colliery, constructed at a time when the industry was expanding but in the event never used, stood for many years as silent memorials to a once great industry.

Thorne itself is dominated by the Early English parish church of St Nicholas with its fine Decorated tower with Peel Hill, the earthworks of a motte and bailey castle, to the north. Sykehouse claims to be the longest village in Yorkshire, stretching for nearly eight miles along the long main street. It is surrounded by a dense pattern of hedged fields used for meadow and pasture, and although many of the hedges may have been planted after the Enclosures, some may date back to medieval or Tudor times.

Fishlake is another village surrounded by a network

of winding lanes and small, medieval hedged fields, contrasting strongly with the 'prairie' landscape which surrounds it. In medieval times, the village was an inland port on the River Don, and the thirteenth century parish church of St Cuthbert reflects this former importance. Originally built by the Normans, the church is reputed to be a resting place of the body of the Northumbrian saint on its way to burial at Durham.

Stainforth, on a former crossing of the River Don, received its market charter from Edward III in 1348, and its ancient market square remains. Stainforth served the villagers of Thorne and the Isle of Axholme who landed their goods here, before hiring horses to complete the journey to Doncaster. This important communications link was maintained by the Stainforth-Keadby Canal which opened in 1797, linking with the River Trent via the Don.

The Decorated tower of St Nicholas's Church, Thorne

St Lawrence's Church, Hatfield

© Ian Carstairs

Interior, St Cuthbert's Church, Fishlake.

FOR PEAT'S SAKE

Peat is the organic material which is left from plants which have died in waterlogged conditions. The absence of oxygen in such an environment leads to the partial decay and partial survival of roots, stems and leaves. Through the accumulation of layers of peat, boggy areas known as mires are formed. The raised mires of Thorne and Hatfield Moors receive only rainwater, and are therefore poor in nutrients. The dominant species are sphagnum mosses, which thrive in such conditions as does a significant range of wetland wildlife, making these sites an internationally-important habitat. And because they preserve undecayed pollen, they are also vitally important for the scientific study of past vegetation and climate change. Originally used on a small scale for fuel for cottage fires, peat is now regrettably, widely used as a garden compost.

CASSON'S GARDEN

Evidence of a unique horticultural venture which briefly existed on the south-western edge of Thorne Moors can still be seen today in the annual flowering of masses of rhododendrons. These are the remains of what was known as 'Casson's Garden', an ambitious nineteenth century project which attracted large numbers of visitors to the area. William Casson was a local Quaker and historian who set up the 'experimental garden' alongside the Thorne Waste Drain in the 1830s, planting it with the then-fashionable rhododendrons, fuchias, heathers and salvias. Visitors in 1842 remarked on the "rare and beautiful flowering shrubs and plants, arbours, alcoves, &c.; it is, in fact, a very oasis all around being peat, turf and bog."

4. Isle of Axholme and the Eastern Levels

The Isle of Axholme has always been a place apart, ever since it *was* virtually an island, surrounded by the seasonal marshes and meres of the landscape before it was drained and enclosed.

It may rise only about 100ft/30m above the surrounding former wetland, but that is enough to make it seem like an entirely different country from the encircling flatlands of the Levels, with the lowlands of the River Trent to the east.

Red brick and pantile-roofed villages such as Haxey – after which the Isle takes its name – are strung like pearls along the A161, which follows the north-south Axholme ridge, and probably follows the course of a prehistoric ridgeway. Clumps of horse chestnut trees, white-candled in spring and bearing bright enamelled 'conkers' in autumn, line the road in stark contrast to the virtually-treeless landscape on either side. The views from the ridge are far-reaching, and there always seems to be a breeze blowing from west or east across these Humberhead 'uplands'. The truncated remains of several former windmills, now sometimes converted into homes, bear evidence to the way that that wind was formerly ultilised.

Evenly spaced along the ridge from the south stand the villages of Haxey, Westwoodside on its spur, Low Burnham, Epworth and Belton, with Owston Ferry on the western bank of the River Trent. Crowle stands proudly isolated on its own hill.

In the north, Eastoft, Luddington, Garthorpe, Fockerby and Adlingfleet are strung out along the course of the former eastern branch of the River Don. At Eastoft, the curiously-wide main street marks the position of the former river channel of the Don, now infilled and faced by rows of houses. The river also marked the county boundary, so the west side of the street was formerly in the West Riding of Yorkshire, and the east side in Lincolnshire.

Some of these villages on the Isle of Axholme still show evidence of narrow medieval strip fields, again in sharp contrast to the vast open prairies in the plain below. These unique and nationally-important field systems are now being protected under a special Countryside Stewardship Special Project in which the Countryside Agency, English Heritage, North Lincolnshire Council and the Rural Development Service of the Department of Farming and Rural Affairs have worked in partnership with local farmers to encourage them to cultivate their crops in the traditional strip pattern.

The Isle is easily the most populous rural part of the Levels, and its history reflects a long period of occupation from prehistoric times onwards. Iron Age people erected fortifications around the sheep-cropped 269ft/82m summit of Gringley Beacon in the far south – incidentally, one of the finest viewpoints in the Levels. The ancient elaborately-carved Viking memorial cross, rescued from use as a door lintel in the Norman parish church of St Oswald at Crowle in 1919,

St Oswald's Church, Crowle

dates from the ninth or tenth centuries.

We actually know the names of several of the earliest Saxon, Norse and Scandinavian settlers on this high ridge, because *Ali* (Althorpe); *Beocca* or *Beohha* (Beckingham); *Eoppa* (Epworth); *Gerulf* (Garthorpe); *Hak* (Haxey); *Hunbald* (Upperthorpe) and *Walhhere*, (Walkeringham) gave their names to their home villages, and are still remembered in modern place-names (see box).

Later the Normans erected a wooden motte and bailey castle to the west of Owston Ferry, an obvious and ancient ferry point across the mighty Trent. This later became known as Kinniard Castle and was refortified by Roger de Mowbray during the revolt against Henry II in 1173-4. It was dismantled under orders from the king in 1174 and never rebuilt, although its earthwork remains still stand next to the parish church, which originated as the castle chapel.

To the north of Owston at Low Melwood Farm are the remains of an important Carthusian priory, now buried within a large moated enclosure. Low Melwood was important as one of a small number of 'charter-houses' in England. The medieval monastic order of the Knight's Templar had a house at Temple Belwood,

The Old Rectory at Epworth

Epworth Market Place, with the Old Court House left

St Andrew's Church, Epworth

to the north of Belton, later the site of a country house which was demolished in the mid-twentieth century. Also north of Belton is Hirst Priory, a small Augustinian 'cell' which was later the site of a small country house and now a country club and golf course.

The western side of the area became part of the royal hunting forest of Hatfield Chase during the Middle Ages, and the fine medieval churches of Epworth,

Haxey, Crowle and Owston were constructed at this time. Through the Mowbray Award of 1360, the lords of the manor of Epworth were bound to provide for the rights of the people of Axholme to use the extensive lowland commons, and were bound not to make any 'approvements' to the waste, moors or woods, which would impair the commoners' rights.

But those rights were completely disregarded 266 years later, when the Dutch engineer, Cornelius Vermuyden, arrived at the invitation of Charles I. He was charged that the 'drowned and surrounded grounds' of Hatfield Chase, Wroot, Finningley and the Isle of Axholme, 'may be laid dry and made useful' and that he should 'make (the) same fit for tillage or pasture.'

Part of the deal was that his 'heirs and assigns' – essentially venture capitalists and known as the Participants – should receive a third of the 'improved' land. Of the 60,000 acres (24,280ha) involved, a third went to Vermuyden and his friends, a third became Crown property, and the remaining third was handed back to the commoners.

St Pancras Church, Wroot, where John Wesley was curate

The Smithy and Heritage Centre, Owston Ferry

Inscribed plaque on the almshouses, Owston Ferry

Vermuyden diverted the River Idle by using an ancient dyke to convey its water into the Trent near Misterton. In the north of the area, he blocked the eastern arm of the Don through Eastoft and embanked the northern arm and enlarged its channel so that it passed into the Aire below Turnbridge. He also put in two new parallel drains which diverted the waters of the Torne to the Trent at Althorpe.

The course of the old River Don, which formerly meandered north east to meet the Trent and formed the ancient county boundary between Yorkshire and Lincolnshire, can still be traced in the modern land-scape, but especially from aerial photographs. The string of villages which used to stand on its banks are Sandtoft, Eastoft, Luddington, Garthorpe and Adlingfleet, and at Eastoft, the bed of the river can still be made out in the middle of the dual carriageway of the main village street.

Millennium clock, Market Place, Owston Ferry

As might be expected, local people, especially those on the Isle of Axholme, were not too happy about these imposed changes, as they were losing valuable meadow land for raising their stock, together with their ancient rights of fishing and wildfowling. As a result, there were frequent attacks on the Participants' banks, sluices and machinery. Violence and rioting took place, and in 1629, their fortified settlement at Sandtoft was burned down. The full story is best told in the anonymous Edwardian novel, *The Manuscript in the Red Box.*

Not surprisingly, given their strong grievances against King Charles and his 'drainers', the Islonians – as natives of the Isle of Axholme are known – were ardent supporters of the Parliamentary cause when the Civil War broke out in 1642.

It was against this rebellious background that John Wesley was born at Epworth in 1703, and later went on to found world Methodism. During an amazing career of evangelism, when it has been estimated that he covered 250,000 miles and preached 45,000 sermons throughout Britain, Wesley became the figurehead of a religion which now has an estimated 70 million follow-ers throughout the world (see box).

Many come to visit the elegant Queen Anne red brick Old Rectory at Epworth – rebuilt after a fire in 1709, which was the Wesleys' home for many years, and where they are shown his favourite chair (with a very low seat – Wesley only stood 5ft 2in), and his portable prayer stool, along with a vast collection of trinkets known as 'Wesleyana.'

The Wesley Memorial Church in the High Street was built in 1889 in memory of John and Charles Wesley, who are depicted in life-sized stained glass profiles in the beautiful chancel window, looking towards their former home of the Old Rectory. Opposite the memorial church is another Victorian red brick Methodist memorial chapel, this one dedicated to Alexander Kilham, also of Epworth, who founded a breakaway Methodist sect in the eighteenth century. It is now a community hall.

In the churchyard of the lovely twelfth century St Andrew's parish church in Epworth, you can see the table-top tomb of Samuel Wesley, John's father, who was rector of Epworth between 1695 and 1735. John Wesley was curate at St Pancras church at Wroot to the west of Epworth, between 1727 and 1729, when his father Samuel was rector there. Having been barred from preaching in Epworth church on a visit in 1742, the indefatigable John delivered his sermon from his father's tomb.

Towards the end of his long life, the man who once said "The world is my parish" wrote: "I rode to Epworth, which I still love beyond most places in the world."

Haxey on its hill, with its prominent water tower, and Westwoodside

THE NORSE LEGACY

Many placenames on and around the Isle of Axholme reflect the Norse or Saxon origins of their first settlers, whose names amazingly are often still recalled in the modern name.

Althorpe – '*Ali's* small village' (Old Norse)

Axholme – 'island of Haxey' (Old Norse)

Beckingham – 'village of *Beocca's* or *Beohha's* people' (Old English)

Belton – 'settlement on dry land in fenny country' (Old Norse)

Beltoft – 'homestead on dry land in fenny country' (Old Norse)

Coney Garth – 'King's or rabbit farm' (Old Norse)

Crowle – 'winding stream' (Old English)

Eastoft – 'homestead by an ash grove' (Old Norse)

East Lound – 'grove or copse east of Graiselound' (Old Norse)

Epworth – '*Eoppa's* enclosure' (Old English)

Garthorpe – '*Gerulf's* small village' (Old Norse)

Graiselound – 'grove or copse with cress' (Old Norse)

Gringley-on-the-Hill – probably 'dwellers on a green hill clearing' (Old English)

Haxey – '*Hak's* island' (Old Norse)

Langholme – 'long island' (Old Norse)

Low Burnham – 'lower settlement on a brook' (Old English)

Misterton – 'settlement of the monastery' (Old English)

Owston Ferry – 'the ferry at the village to the east (of Epworth)' (Old Scandinavian)

Sandtoft – 'sandy homestead' (Old Norse)

Upperthorpe – '*Hunbald's* small village' (Old Scandinavian)

Walkeringham – 'village of *Walhhere's* people' (Old English)

Westwoodside – 'west wood side' (Old English)

West and East Butterwick – 'western and eastern butter or dairy farm' (Old English)

Wroot – 'spur of land resembling a pig's snout' (Old English)

THE WESLEY DYNASTY

The founders of the Wesley dynasty were Samuel and Susanna, who were both children of ministers who had been ejected from their parishes for not conforming to the established church. Susanna, who exerted an enormous influence on her children, especially John, was a particularly vehement opponent of the divine right of kings, whereas Samuel, rector of Epworth, was a traditional non-Catholic High Churchman.

Their sons John and Charles, the co-founders of Methodism, were baptised as were all the Wesley's 10 surviving children, in the parish church of St Andrew's. John was educated at Charterhouse and Oxford, where he became a member of the radical 'Holy Club.' After their father's death in 1735, he and Charles set out on what was to prove an unsuccessful mission to Georgia in what was then the British colony of North America. After a famous revelation in an Aldersgate Street chapel in London, John embarked on his astonishing peripatetic evangelical career. Charles is perhaps best remembered as the writer of a collection of rousing Methodist hymns.

5. The North

Market day on a Monday in Selby is a colourful affair. The covered stalls of the traders fill the cramped space of the Market Place in front of the sparkling white limestone Norman façade of the West Front of the Abbey church of St Mary and St Germain.

The hustle and bustle of jostling shoppers in the market adds life and movement to the scene, as they have for perhaps eight centuries. The view is the epitome of what most people think of as an English country market town.

Yet Selby's magnificent Abbey – recently described by Simon Jenkins as "a stately old lady, retired to the country with her dignity and memories intact" – has survived fire and flood, sinking foundations and

Selby Market, with the Abbey in the background

falling towers, the Dissolution and vandalism by Cromwell's zealots.

Founded in 1069 by Benedict of Auxerre, it was the first Benedictine monastery in the north of England, and the one crucial event which established Selby's future. To put that date into its historical context, it was just three years after the last victory of Anglo-Saxon England by Harold at the Battle of Stamford Bridge just 15 miles away, and the last successful invasion of the country by William the Conqueror at Hastings 19 days later.

Benedict's first monastery was a humble, wooden affair founded on a bend on the west bank of the river after Benedict had received a vision that he should set up a monastery there, bringing with him the middle finger of St Germain's right hand as the precious relict necessary to attract pilgrims.

Taking time off from his infamous 'Harrying of the North' – the vicious act of ethnic cleansing following a local uprising during which it is thought that as many as 100,000 people were put to the sword – William the Conqueror celebrated Christmas at York in 1069. He may even have met Benedict there, but certainly sanctioned the setting-up of the monastery at Selby, perhaps as an act of expiation. Whatever the truth, there is a longstanding local tradition that his queen Maltilda gave birth to their youngest son, later Henry I, while staying at Selby.

When the saintly Abbot Hugh succeeded Benedict

in 1097, he resolved to rebuild the abbey in stone, 150 yards/136m further away from the river. Originally, there were rumours that the abbey would be moved to a completely different, less flood-prone, location away from Selby, but Henry I, perhaps in recognition of his birthplace, refused permission.

Norman doorway and the west end of Selby Abbey

This twelfth century rebuilding gave us the abbey church very much as we see it today, and the massive round patterned Norman columns in the nave and rib vaulting which are so similar to those of Durham Cathedral that many authorities believe that they must have employed the same architect. One is still named Hugh's Pillar.

Further rebuilding took place in the thirteenth, fourteenth and fifteenth centuries, but the monastery suffered the fate of all others when it was dissolved by Henry VIII in 1539. Previously, it had been a head-quarters of the leaders of the ill-fated Pilgrimage of Grace, which had opposed the Dissolution.

The abbey church was made the parish church of Selby in 1618, and seems to have escaped the worst of the reformers during the Civil War. But in 1690, the effects of its shallow foundations, originally built on sand and beams of wood just three feet (1m) above the water table, resulted in the catastrophic collapse of the central tower. The church remained in this partly ruinous state for many years until Sir George Gilbert Scott's restoration in 1871.

Then a disastrous fire struck in 1906, turning the stately central tower into a chimney, and melting the bells and lead roof, which poured down the nave in streams of silver. The final restoration, including new upper stages of the tower and south transept, took place a year later. A continuous programme of more recent renovation, notably aided by lottery players through the Heritage Lottery Fund, has given the abbey its present sparkling appearance.

Selby had been a successful port on the Ouse for Yorkshire woollens and other products since medieval times, but it was the construction of the swing bridge in 1791-2 which really opened up the town. The coming of the main line Doncaster-York railway in

1871 further confirmed the commercial importance of the town.

Howden, just a dozen miles away to the east, is another ancient market town founded around its superb church, the collegiate minster of St Peter and Paul. There's another Durham connection here, as William the Conqueror gave the original Saxon church and manor of Howden to William of St Calais, the Bishop of Durham, in 1080. It still remains under the rule of the Benedictine Cathedral Priory of Durham, although in the diocese of York.

The magnificent 135-foot/41m Early English tower, so reminiscent of Durham's, dominates the sleepy and well-preserved little market town which in the nineteenth century was the home of the largest horse fair in Britain, attracting buyers from all over Europe. It had been granted the right to hold a fair by King John as long ago as 1200.

The church is mainly in the Early English style, but the nave and the now partly-ruinous choir was rebuilt in the fashionable Decorated style in 1267. Unlike its neighbour at Selby, the church escaped the ravages of

Howden Minster from the churchyard

Goole, showing water towers and dockside cranes

Henry VIII's Dissolution of the Monasteries in the sixteenth century, but as a collegiate church, it fell victim to the suppression of colleges in Edward VI's reign. Like many other churches, it suffered at the hands of troops during the Civil War. After the Dissolution, the large church was simply beyond the means of the parish, and finally, the roof of the chancel, choir and eastern end of the church collapsed in a thunderstorm in 1696 and were never rebuilt.

Highlights inside the church today include the gloomy Saltmarshe Chantry, with its timeworn medieval effigies of members of the Saltmarshe and Metham families, and the magnificent and rare stone pulpitum or stone screen which separated the collegiate east end from the parochial west. Don't miss the 1664 parish coffin in the Saltmarshe Chantry, used to carry those who could not afford their own to the grave.

Another busy port is Goole, on the south bank of the Ouse. Goole was little more than a hamlet by the side of the Ouse in the 1820s. The Dutch River – one of Vermuyden's attempts at drainage – had been constructed at a cost of £30,000 in 1633 between the River

Bishop of Durham's Manor House, Howden

Selby was a sea-port town
When Goole was but a marsh,
Now Goole it is a sea-port town
And Selby fares the worse!

Goole has managed to retain and expand its trade, especially with Europe, and despite being 40 miles from the sea, it is today still one of the busiest container ports in the country, aided no doubt by the construction of the nearby M62 and M18. More recently it has become a major centre for car and timber imports, in addition to other charter vessels.

The area to the north-east of Selby in the valley of the Derwent has always been low-lying and subject to winter flooding. As Henry VIII's chaplain and antiquary, John Leland, described it in 1520: "This ryver at Greate Raynes ragith and overfloweth, much of the ground there aboute being low meadows."

'Ings' is a common name in these parts, and it means 'land belonging to the people' or common land, which was often poor quality, low-lying meadows subject to seasonal flooding. The Lower Derwent Valley National Nature Reserve is a mosaic of over 1,000 acres/404ha of haymeadow and pasture set in traditionally-farmed

Don at Newbridge to the Ouse to try to solve serious flood and drainage problems caused by Vermuden's earlier works. In 1826, the Aire and Calder Navigation was opened linking the Ouse with Knottingley, and Goole quickly became the hub of a waterway network.

Coal from the West Yorkshire coalfield was the most important product, and at the height of the trade, up to 1½ million tons annually were exported through Goole. The canal 'undertakers' built the great landmark which is the parish church of St John between 1843-48, and the grant of a weekly market – one of the last to be given – was obtained, as the town expanded rapidly. Among its more modern buildings, it still retains some fascinating and rare Victorian machinery, like the coal-handling gear and the 'Tom Pudding' Hoist. This is a unique late nineteenth century structure, now part of the Goole Waterways Museum, which dominates the skyline and was designed to hoist coal-barges (known as 'Tom Puddings') and empty them into ships.

During the mid-nineteenth century, the population of Goole finally overtook that of Selby, and local people coined the following sarcastic ditty:

Howden Market Place

Thorpe Marsh Power Station, Barnby Dun

grasslands. Running for over 12 miles between Newton-upon-Derwent and Wressle, these lowland water meadows show us a landscape which was once common in Britain and Europe, but which is now quite rare. They were created by centuries of traditional grazing and haymaking, and local people supplemented their incomes by wildfowling on the abundant birdlife which still overwinter on the ings, to the delight of modern birdwatchers, who can use hides and other facilities at Bank Island, Wheldrake Ings and North Duffield Carrs.

A notable landmark hereabouts is Wressle Castle, built around 1380 by Sir Thomas Percy, but an impressive and rare survival of a medieval castle, with two towers and a curtain wall surviving in remarkably good condition despite being damaged in a siege during the Civil War. Wressle Castle is private and not open to the public.

But the major landmarks in the Humberhead Levels north of the River Ouse and the M62 motorway are undoubtedly the massive power stations at Eggborough, Drax and, just outside the area, at Ferrybridge on the A1, which feed electricity into the National Grid via a network of pylons strung out

Wressle Castle

across the countryside.

Alternative energy has not been ignored in this part of the Levels, and under the title of 'Project Arbre', the first wood-fuelled power station in Britain was built at Eggborough. To provide fuel for the new station, considerable planting of short-rotation coppice willow has taken place in the surrounding countryside, perhaps pointing towards a future where society moves towards more sustainably-produced electricity.

Overshadowed by the huge cooling towers of the Drax power station, the slender spire of St Mary's Church, Hemingbrough, rises 180 feet above the flat countryside. Since it was built before the Norman Conquest, St Mary's has been added to by successive generations, and contains some particularly fine medieval woodwork.

The villages of Sherburn in Elmet and Church Fenton, in the extreme west of the area, are inescapably linked with the fortunes of the former RAF fighter station of Church Fenton. The suffix 'in Elmet' recalls the Anglo-Saxon Kingdom of Elmet, which covered much of the present day county of West Yorkshire, but later applied to the name of the Norse administrative area or 'wapentake'.

Drax Power Station

6. Wildlife of the Levels

(The bog was…) trembling in waves when you jumped on its…surface, till the undulations were lost in the distance or at the edge of the nearest ditch. No man could traverse these water cuts…without 'fen boards', for less than five minutes would have sunk the strongest swimmer overhead in black, oozy peat about eleven feet deep.

Rev Adrian Woodruffe-Peacock, quoted in
Catherine Caufield's *Thorne Moors*

This account of Thorne Moors by Woodruffe-Peacock, a Lincolnshire vicar and nineteenth century naturalist, describes perfectly walking across the quaking surface of a raised bog – a weird, earth-shaking sensation you can still experience in certain parts of Thorne and Hatfield Moors.

The moors are a very rare example of such a habitat, once widespread in post-glacial Britain. According to official government figures, about 96 per cent of Britain's raised bogs have now been drained, excavated for their peat, or otherwise destroyed. On an international scale, they are Britain's equivalent of the Amazonian rainforest; an ecological gem, and one of the nation's most important areas for its natural history.

Five thousand years ago, most of the Humberhead Levels were covered in dense woodland of pine, lime, oak, hazel and ash. Some small incursions were made by prehistoric people, but the forest which blanketed the area grew and regenerated naturally for hundreds of years.

Antiquary John Leland, chaplain to Henry VIII and keeper of his library, described the hunting forest in his *Itinerary of England and Wales* between 1530-40 thus:

The quarters about Heathfield be forest ground, and though wood be scars there yet there is plentie of red deer, that haunt the fennes and great mores.

Evidence of that ancient, impenetrable wildwood can still be found in the 'paludified' timber – known as 'bog oaks' – which still frequently can be seen emerging from the peat bogs or from nearby farmland, where it is dragged out and dumped at the edge of fields or by the roadside. The peat grew so quickly that it swallowed-up and engulfed anything that fell into it. With the almost complete disappearance of Britain's primeval wildwood – an even rarer habitat than raised boglands – the preserved trees of Thorne and Hatfield Moors also constitute a precious record of the ancient forests of this country and the rest of Europe.

What caused the sudden incursion of the marshes and bogs and the destruction of the forest is still being debated by ecologists, but one theory is that prehistoric

The flooded Derwent Ings attracts thousands of wildfowl in the winter

people over-exploited the resource and cut down most of the trees around 4000 years ago, creating the conditions under which the moors formed.

Today they are the country's largest remaining examples of lowland raised peat bogs, described by Catherine Caufield as "lying on the landscape like huge raindrops, in apparent defiance of the laws of gravity", and one of its most important nature conservation sites.

After a long campaign by conservationists like William Bunting (see box), many years of damaging mechanical peat extraction, which was gradually eating away this precious resource, should end in 2010. The 12-square-mile/3,318ha of Thorne, Hatfield, Goole and Crowle Moors, includes a large area of abandoned peat cuttings which is now managed by English Nature as the Humberhead Peatlands National Nature Reserve (NNR). This includes parts of Crowle Moor

Cotton grass growing in old peat cuttings, Thorne Moors

View from the Willow Pool hide, Potteric Carr Nature Reserve

which is owned and managed by the Lincolnshire Wildlife Trust.

According to Jeremy Purseglove, writing in his *Taming the Flood* (1988):

Hatfield Chase resembles the wildest and most exciting heathy common …Among the glittering ranks of silver birch, from which project the creamy brackets of polypore and tinder fungus, the mysterious nightjar churrs to his mate.

More than 5,000 species of plants and animals, including some of Britain's rarest and most endangered species and over 4,800 species of insects alone, live on Thorne Moors. Nearly 200 species of birds have been recorded there, and 75 use the area for nesting, including up to 50 pairs of the nationally-rare nightjar mentioned by Purseglove. This makes it a breeding site of international importance for this strange,

Large heath butterflies on cottongrass

nocturnal, hawk-like insect-feeder. Other breeding birds include teal, snipe, whinchat and tree pipit.

Standing on the border between lowland and upland Britain, the area is also home to a number of species on their northern or southern limits. An example of this is that silver-voiced migrant, the secretive nightingale, which is at one of its northernmost limits in Britain here. Other southern examples at their northern limit include the reed damsel-bug and the marsh pea.

Northern types at their southern limit include the twite, and the large heath butterfly, whose caterpillars live and hibernate in dense tussocks of cottongrass which are found on Thorne and Crowle Moors. Summer visitors include the dashing marsh harrier and the smaller hobby, which feeds on smaller birds and dragon-

Heather in flower on Hatfield Moors

Cross-leaved heath, Thorne Moors

flies, which are often taken acrobatically in mid-flight. Over-wintering birds include the wraith-like hen harrier, the kestrel-sized merlin and the short-eared owl.

There is a sizeable population of Britain's most common and only poisonous snake, the adder (locally-known as a 'hetherd') on the moors, and their flesh boiled in a broth was once recommended as a cure for leprosy, scurvy, rheumatism, consumption and tuberculosis. Many local residents, including the indefatigable William Bunting (see box), have made an income from catching adders, or vipers, either for the medical properties of their flesh, or for their use in research or feeding mongooses at London Zoo! Under the latest wildlife legislation, adders are a protected species.

Female adder

Among the 4,800 species of insects found here are the unique mire pill beetle, once thought to be extinct and known only from the fossil record; the Thorne Moor ground beetle; the three-inch-long giant raft spider and the amusingly nick-named 'hairy canary' fly (see box).

The other internationally-important wildlife site in the Humberhead Levels is the Lower Derwent Valley National Nature Reserve. Stretching 12 miles between Newton-upon-Derwent and Wressle, the reserve is an example of another kind of landscape – winter-flooding lowland meadows – which was once common in Britain and Europe but which is now extremely rare.

The Ings are a patchwork of about 2,500 acres/1012ha of carefully-managed haymeadow and pasture set in intensive arable farmland. They were created by over 1,000 years of

Round-leaved sundew growing on bog moss

A flock of wigeon rise from Ellerton Ings

traditional grazing and haymaking, and for many centuries, local people like the splendidly-named Snowdon Slights made a living by wildfowling on the abundant birdlife which overwinter on the Ings. White-bearded Slights, his faithful gun dog at his side, was a regular sight at places like East Cottingwith Ings, where he shot wildfowl using a punt gun during the winter, and fished in the summer.

During the spring and summer, wading birds like the curlew, redshank, snipe and lapwing nest in the flower-filled meadows, marshes and ditches, while in autumn and winter, huge flocks of teal, shoveler, wigeon, and Bewick's and whooper swans arrive from the Arctic to spend the winter in the flooded, low-lying landscape.

If the Ings are a managed, natural landscape, then Potteric Carr, a Yorkshire Wildlife Trust reserve south of Doncaster, is a man-made landscape which provides many social and environmental benefits close

Bog rosemary, Thorne Moors

to the city. It is another good illustration of the dynamic landscape change and new beginnings which are taking place in the Levels. Habitats at Potteric include reedy wetland 'flashes' created by coal mining subsidence which are rich in breeding wildfowl like shoveler, pochard and tufted duck, and the rare garganey, and old railway yards slowly being recolonised by Nature. The wet areas and standing water encourage a huge range of insects, among which dragonflies are especially important and spectacular examples.

Skipwith Common north of Selby is one of the last remaining areas of lowland heath in the north of England. This 667 acre/270ha nature reserve is managed by the Escrick Park Estate through an agreement with English Nature, and features a half-mile/1 km long nature trail through the heathland and heather.

46

Whooper swan taking off

© Terry Weston

THE 'HAIRY CANARY'

Discovered on Thorne Moors in 1985 and Hatfield Moors in 1991 by Peter Skidmore, former Keeper of Natural Sciences at Doncaster Museum, this locally-common but nationally extremely-rare *Muscidae* fly has only been found in two other places in Britain. The fly, scientific name *Phaonia jaroschewskii*, obtained its popular name from an article by Mr Skidmore in the *Thorne and Hatfield Moors Papers* when he used its presence as an indicator, like the coal miners' gas-detecting canaries, of the imminent threat to the wetlands. It has bright yellow legs, and a very hairy abdomen and legs. It is usually found in tropical locations, where it is a parasite on the desert locust.

© Peter Skidmore

WILLIAM BUNTING (1916-1995)

Amateur naturalist William Bunting is the man who is credited with the almost single-handed salvation of what is left of Thorne and Hatfield Moors by his vigorous and outspoken campaigning. In her dedication to *Thorne Moors*, Catherine Caufield described Bunting as a 'naturalist pamphleteer, archivist, rebel, bad-tempered old sod, and inspiration'. The son of a Barnsley greengrocer, Bunting came to Thorne after the Second World War and instantly fell in love with the moors, fighting tirelessly in the courts to save them from gradual destruction by peat extraction. In 1972, he led a guerrilla group known as 'Bunting's Beavers' which conducted a campaign of direct action by damming the drains excavated by Fisons Ltd near the Dutch Canal, which were threatening to lower the water table to a disastrously-low level. While some may not have agreed with his direct action tactics, Bunting's tireless efforts in championing the moors undoubtedly were instrumental in their salvation.

© John Hartley

William Bunting

7. A Humberhead Timeline

Early Prehistory   **10,000-4,000 years ago**

The first hunter-gathers move across the land bridge from the Continent onto the Humberhead Levels, following the retreat of the Ice Age ice sheet. Scant evidence of them is revealed in scatters of flint found in places like Moorends, Sutton Common and at Misterton Carr, near the Isle of Axholme. The landscape is heavily-wooded with lime, oak and hazel trees and numerous wild food plants and animals such as deer, beaver and predatory wolves.

Bronze Age   **4,000-3,000 years ago**

Bronze Age burial mounds are found on the higher and drier ground which surround the wetlands of the Levels, such as on the Yorkshire Wolds. A wooden trackway dated to the Bronze Age was found under peat deposits on Thorne Moors in 1971. Ritual deposits of artefacts such as bronze axes and spearheads in the Trent Valley, and evidence of the use of rivers for transport is confirmed by the discovery of well-preserved dug-out boats or canoes from North Lincolnshire and the River Trent, upstream from the Humberhead Levels.

Iron Age   **3,000-2,000 years ago**

More evidence of the use of rivers into the Iron Age was the find of the Hasholme logboat found in 1984 in the Foulness Valley north of the Humber. More recently, a spectacular chariot burial was discovered at Ferrybridge near the A1(M), indicating a high status burial. Various iron-working sites have been discovered in the Foulness area, but the major Iron Age site in the region is at Sutton Common, where two large embanked enclosures have been investigated. The latest thinking is that this 'marsh fort' may have been used for the storage of grain.

Romans   **2,000 years ago**

The Romans probably came into the Humberhead Levels in the late 70s AD and established a major settlement at Doncaster (*Danum*) and a fort at Roall on the River Aire. Roman roads ring the region, with that from Lincoln to York passing through Doncaster and the road connecting Lincoln with York via the Humber following the edge of the Wolds. Roman bridges have been discovered at Scaftworth on the Idle and at Rossington on the Torne and major pottery sites at Cantley, Rossington, Holme-on-Spalding Moor.

Anglo-Saxon and Viking   **2,000-1,000 years ago**

During the frequent struggles for supremacy between the Anglo-Saxon kingdoms, there are traditions of a major battle between Raewald, King of the East Angles and Aethelfrith of Northumbria in 'Hatfield-land' in 616; and in 633, Penda of Mercia defeated Eadwine of Northumberland also at Hatfield. An important possibly royal Anglo-Saxon settlement has been excavated at Flixborough on the Trent, and placename evidence

Time Team's *Victor Ambrus's impression of what the Sutton Common 'marsh fort' might have looked like*

(such as Haxey, Axholme, Sandtoft and Eastoft) also shows the strong Scandinavian presence in the area. The Crowle Stone in the nave of St Oswald's Church, Crowle, is decorated in the Viking style and is thought to be the shaft of a memorial cross dating from the tenth century.

Normans   1000-1200AD

Domesday Book (1086) records several settlements in area of the Humberhead Levels, mainly on higher, drier sites, such as the Isle of Axholme and at Hatfield, Fishlake, Stainforth and Thorne. The latter villages were all part of the Manor of Conisbrough, awarded by William I to his son-in-law William de Warenne, who built the first motte and bailey castle at Conisbrough. Other motte and bailey castles were erected at Tickhill, Thorne and Owston Ferry. Hatfield Chase, a 270-square-mile unenclosed hunting forest, is established for the entertainment of the Norman overlords. The magnificent Abbey at Selby, founded by Benedict in

The superb Norman doorway at St Cuthbert's Church, Fishlake

1069, is rebuilt by Hugh in the early twelfth century.

Middle Ages 1200-1400
In addition to Wressle Castle, the most important late Medieval fortified palace in the Levels, over 100 moated sites (such as those at West Cowick and Wood Hall) are constructed during the thirteenth century to enclose and defend high status sites, such as manor houses and monasteries. The ancient field systems around Fishlake are laid out. Monasteries are established, including Drax and Selby on the Ouse and at Thorganbury on the Derwent, and the Archbishop of Durham sets up his palace at Howden. The Mowbray Award of 1360 sets down the rights of Isle of Axholme residents to common land on the moors.

Motte and bailey castle, Thorne

Conisbrough Castle

Tudors and Stuarts 1400-1700
Successive monarchs and other nobility use Hatfield Chase for hunting after it becomes royal property. The most famous hunt, recorded by a contemporary painting, is that attended by Prince Henry, James I's elder son, in 1609 on Thorne Mere. After serious flooding in the area, Charles I calls in Cornelius Vermuyden in 1626 to undertake the first comprehensive drainage of the area, and he brings in large numbers of French and Dutchmen, or 'Participants', to undertake the work. William Bradford of Austerfield, joins the Pilgrim Fathers on the *Mayflower* and becomes governor of Plymouth County in Massachusetts. Local people protest and support Parliament during the Civil Wars, while the landowning gentry mostly support the King.

Industrial Revolution 1700-1850
Turnpike roads are constructed throughout the area, linking the main market towns which were rebuilt in fashionable styles – often in brick. John Wesley, born at Epworth in 1703, breaks away from the Church of England to form Methodism. At Askern, the lord of the

Ancient strip fields, near Epworth

Manor, Viscount Galway, and Humphrey Osbaldeston erect a stone building in 1794 over the site of the mineral spa. Steam power is introduced for the first time to power the pumps draining the levels, and in 1826 a new canal is cut from Goole to Knottingley, now known as the Aire and Calder Navigation. The Railway Age dawns with the construction of the East Coast main line through Doncaster in 1871.

Victorian Britain   1850-1900

The Isle of Axholme is connected to the rail system by the Goole and Marshland Railway in 1898-1900, and the Axholme Joint Railway in 1905, linked with the main line at Haxey. At the same time, tourism is boosted by the popularity of the health spa at Askern, which begins to rival that at Harrogate. The Hatfield Chase Corporation, establishing a board of drainage

Tomb of Samuel Wesley, Epworth churchyard

The Victorian redbrick pumping station at Dirtness, near Sandtoft

commissioners, is set up in 1862. Commercial peat extraction for horse litter starts on Thorne and Hatfield Moors in the 1880s under the Thorne Improvement Company.

Modern Britain   1900-to date

Coal mining had arrived in the area at Conisbrough in 1894, and the sinking of pits moved steadily east until the Selby coalfield development of the 1970s. Today, however, few pits are still in operation. The British Moss Litter Company continues to extract peat commercially, to be sold as animal bedding and a replacement for garden compost. Peat extraction, which has been carried on on a small scale since medieval times, becomes fully mechanised in 1963 when Fisons acquire the company. Production will cease, for environmental reasons, in 2010. Thorne Moors was created a Site of Special Scientific Interest (SSSI) in 1970 and later became part of the Humberhead Peatlands National Nature Reserve. The road and rail lifting bridge across the Trent is built at Keadby – then the largest in the world. As the branch railway lines close during the 1960s, 70s and 80s, they are replaced by the M62, M18 and M180 motorways.

HATFIELD CHASE

Hatfield Chase, covering about 80,000 acres/ 72,850ha, was established by William the Conqueror as an unenclosed hunting preserve for the nobility shortly after the Conquest in 1066. It was administered by his son-in-law William de Warenne, who built the first castle at Conisbrough. On the death of de Warenne, it reverted to the Crown, but it was not subject to Forest Law until 1460, in the reign of Edward IV. Several royal hunts were held there, the last recorded of which was in 1609 and shown in the famous painting of Thorne Mere, when Prince Henry, son of James I, and a party comprising 100 boats rounded up 500 deer before slaughtering them.

SOME KEY HISTORICAL FIGURES

Anglo Saxon and Viking: Eadwine, king of Northumbria, who had a palace at Hatfield and who was defeated there in battle by Penda of Mercia in 633.

Norman: William de Warenne, son-in-law of William the Conqueror, builder of the first Conisburgh Castle and governor of the hunting forest of Hatfield Chase; **Hamelin Plantagenet**, fifth Earl of Surrey, who built Conisbrough keep, and **Hugh**, builder of Selby Abbey.

Middle Ages: John de Mowbray, who had a mansion at Epworth, author of the Mowbray Award setting out the rights of commoners,

Tudors and Stuarts: Cornelius Vermuyden, Dutch drainage engineer charged by Charles I to drain the southern part of the Humberhead Levels in 1626. **Abraham de Pryme**, descendant of a Dutch settler, local historian and curate at Hatfield in 1696. **John Wesley**, founder of Methodism, born at Epworth in 1703.

Victorian: Thomas Crapper, inventor of the flushing water closet, was born in 1836 at Waterside, near Thorne. He provided Queen Victoria and other members of the royal family with their palace plumbing facilities, and died in London in 1910.

Modern: William Bunting (1916-1995), naturalist and outspoken campaigner for the protection and conservation of Thorne and Hatfield Moors, who lived at Thorne.

Statue of William Bradford at Plymouth, Massachusetts

An aerial view of a flooded Thorne Moors in 1997, showing old peat workings

8. Culture and Customs

If you visit Haxey, a pleasant village situated off the A161 between Misterton and Epworth on St John's Eve (January 6, or the twelfth day of Christmas), you may wonder if you have wandered into a mad-house. For this is the day of the historic game of the Haxey Hood, described as 'Britain's oldest tussle' when, according to one participant, the youth of Haxey and neighbouring Westwoodside "goes mad."

Flooded peat workings on Thorne Moors, Drax steaming in the background

Legend has it that on St John's Eve around 600 years ago, the wife of the lord of the manor Sir John de Mowbray lost her big red hood in a gust of wind as she was out riding over Haxey Hill. She immediately sent 13 'boggans' – people from the surrounding fenlands – chasing after it, and rewarded the country fool who found it and the others half an acre of land in return for the promise that they re-enact the event every year.

The modern Haxey Hood game starts with some serious drinking in the local pubs, and then moves to the Mounting Cross outside the east end of the church. Here the 'Fool' is grabbed by the 12 Boggans (the name given to the referees or game officials) and placed on the cross base. There he gives warnings about rough play, avoiding damage, and injuring others. He then gives the Fool's traditional cry of:-

Hoose agen hoose, toon agen toon;

If tha meets a man, nok 'im doon but doan't 'urt 'im

Which translated means "House against house, town against town; if you meet a man, knock him down but don't hurt him." The Fool is then 'smoked' over a fire of damp straw lit round the base of the cross and leads the large group of men and boys and occasionally girls which make up the 'Sway' into the fields surrounding the village. The Fool is accompanied by the Boggans, who are dressed like Morris Men in red jumpers, and the Chief Boggan, who is dressed in a hunting pink coat and a top hat decorated with flowers and badges.

Accompanying him is the Lord of the Hood, also in hunting pink with a top hat decorated with flowers and pheasant feathers, who carries the Sway Hood. This is a three-foot length of thick heavy rope encased and sewn into a leather tube. He also has his 'magic' willow wand of office which consists of twelve willow wands tied together with one more turned upside

The Sway Hood is held aloft

The main scrum of the Haxey Hood game

down in the centre. These are then bound round with 13 more willow twigs tied up with a red ribbon.

This is said to represent the sword and the blood from when this game was played with a bullock's head

56

after it had been slaughtered and beheaded. In an obvious Christianisation of what was probably an originally pagan custom, the willows are also said to represent the twelve Apostles and the thirteenth in the centre, Judas. The Fool leads the crowd to the middle of a field and starts proceedings by throwing 12 'running hoods'. These are rolled-up and sewn hessian sacks tied round with red ribbons. The youngsters in the crowd run for them, and the first two or three are stopped by the Boggans on the edge of the field and the hoods returned to the Lord.

After this has warmed up the crowd, the Sway Hood is thrown up and the main scrum – by this time consisting of dozens of heaving and steaming bodies – converges on the hood and the sway starts in earnest. The aim is to get the hood into one of the public houses in Haxey or Westwoodside, where it is soaked in beer and then hung over the bar until the following year. The game can last for three or four hours, but despite some very rough and muddy scrummages, there are usually very few injuries and little damage. Any damage is repaired the next day and most injuries come from exhaustion or bruises from the sway or too much beer before or after the game, whether it be the winners celebrating or the losers drowning their sorrows.

Another annual custom at Haxey is the Easter 'Candle Auction', when strips of land known as 'meres' in the ancient open fields are auctioned off to rent for haymaking. The auction is overseen by the 'Townsmen' – the successors to the villagers who have been managing the common fields since the early Middle Ages. Pins are stuck into a candle and the last bid made before the pin falls is the winning one.

A boggart is the local name for a ghost, the most famous of which in the Humberhead Levels is Old Jeffrey, who haunted the Old Vicarage at Epworth (see box). Regular ghost walks are held for visitors during the summer season at Epworth.

A purely Christian legend is that of the dedication of the parish church of Fishlake to St Cuthbert. It is recorded that when Cuthbert, Bishop of Lindisfarne and favourite saint of Northumbria, died in 687 he was buried on Holy Island, but his body was exhumed two centuries later when the priory was threatened by Viking raiders.

There followed seven years of almost constant movement of the sacred remains, as the oak coffin was transferred from church to church throughout northern England to avoid the wrath of the Vikings. It reached its final resting place in Durham's magnificent Norman cathedral in 995, and Cuthbert's posthumous journey was over.

Traditionally one of these temporary resting places was Fishlake, hence the unusual dedication, and the beautiful twelfth century church with its superbly-decorated Norman west door perhaps signifies the builders' acknowledgement of its ecclesiastical importance.

Wildfowling on Derwent Ings

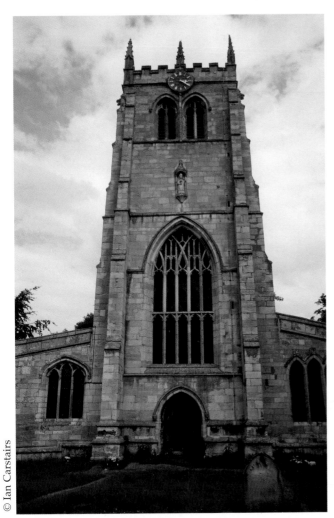

© Ian Carstairs

St Cuthbert's Church, Fishlake

guided heritage trail takes the visitor around the area.

Another unique landform in the Thorne area, on the South or Sand Moors to the east of the village, is the way that the peat moors have been divided into a multitude of thin strips – known locally as 'cables' – each bounded by drainage dykes. These are the result of plots of land being gradually extended in ever-lengthening strips as the peat was removed and the ground beneath cultivated. Each 'cable' was owned by its own farm, which are situated in a line along the minor road which runs between The Willows in the north and Orchard Farm to the south, across the Sheffield and South Yorkshire Canal.

The edge of the moorland was gradually extended further away from the town until it met the Thorne Waste Drain, constructed in 1815, which effectively barred further progress of the 'cable' reclamation to the north west. The southern boundary was the Sheffield and South Yorkshire Navigation and the Stainforth and Keadby Canal.

Willows standing in floodwater at Ellerton Ings

The intricate system of small fields and winding lanes around Fishlake date mainly from the period of the Georgian enclosures, and stand out in stark contrast to the broad expanses of the open moor around. Their survival is mainly due to land owner-ship and the drainage of the relatively wet land. A self-

Mention has already been made of warping, the deliberate flooding of farmland to leave silt from the rivers Trent and Ouse to create a rich, fertile soil. This usually took place during the winter between November and May and was a well-regulated and carefully-controlled operation.

The practice of warping became increasingly important from the early years of the nineteenth century, as a way of improving the fertility of low-lying land, especially peatlands. Before 1850, all peatlands up to three miles/5km west of the Trent were being warped in addition to another 3,000 acres/1,200ha east of the river.

For successful warping to take place, a controllable channel was needed which connected to the main tidal rivers, the Trent or the Ouse. Some channels, such as the Swinefleet Warping Drain, had to be specially constructed for this.

A strong embankment was built around a rectangular area of land, known as a warping compartment, which was located alongside a warping drain. The slopes of the compartment had to be very precisely graded, and access of water to the compartment was closely controlled by the operation of sluice gates.

The secret of success in warping lay in allowing the incoming water to spread quickly and evenly over the land, leaving a uniform deposit. About 0.13ins/3.5mm of warp would be left with each tide, and under ideal conditions, about 23-35in/60-90cm would result from a year's operation, although up to four years might be required to reach this depth on higher land.

It is believed that the last warping to be carried out in the Hatfield-Axholme area was just before the First World War at Crowle, and the last warping on Humberside took place at Yokefleet in 1948.

THE TRENT EAGRE

The Severn Bore is a well-known natural phenomenon which occurs in the estuary of the River Severn in the south-west of England. Less well known is the Eagre (also known as the Aegir or Aegre), a similar event which takes place every spring in the River Trent. The funnel-shaped channel of the river is responsible for the phenomenon, which occurs when a high spring tide pushes the heavier salt water from the North Sea underneath the fresh water of the river in a wedge shape, causing a wave which can be 5ft-6ft/1.5m-1.8m high and which travels as far as 34 miles/56km up the Trent.

© Chris Etchells

OLD JEFFREY

Old Jeffrey is the best-known boggart – or ghost – in the area. He is thought to have been a local suicide who haunted the attic of the Old Rectory at Epworth, specifically between December 1716 and February 1717, while the Wesley family were in residence. He manifested himself by mournful groans and knocking on doors and walls throughout the house. This was followed by the sound of breaking glass, footsteps on the landings and a noise like a gobbling turkey. Samuel Wesley believed he was a harbinger of bad tidings, and his son, John, remained fascinated by the haunting for all his life, publishing an account of it in the *Arminian Magazine*.

9. Humberhead Products

The sight of huge fields of the mustard-yellow flowers of oilseed rape is a common one in the Humberhead Levels, sometimes giving the impression of the landscape of a child's colouring book.

But how many people realise that the earliest version of the crop – then known as coleseed – was introduced by the Dutchmen who first drained Thorne and Hatfield Moors in the seventeenth century? These crops are not referred to in pre-drainage records, so the chances are that it was the Dutchmen who introduced them. A political paper written by Sir John Maynard in 1646 complained: "What is coleseed and rape, they are but Dutch commodities and but trash and trumpery."

The name derives from colza, a valuable source of lamp oil until the introduction of mineral-based oils. The streets of Wisbech in Cambridgeshire were being lit by colza oil as early as 1588. Originally grown as a fodder crop, the modern strains of oilseed rape introduced in the 1970s and 80s are varieties of the same species, but it is now used almost exclusively as a cooking oil.

Another crop which was extensively gown in the reclaimed levels was hemp, which had been an important crop in England since the fourteenth century, and was sold at the famous Gainsborough Hemp Market. Later on, hemp crops were replaced by flax, another crop which has seen a recent revival. It was sown in May and pulled at the end of June, and the 'retting' or

Selby Market in full swing

Locally-grown produce on sale at a farmers' market

soaking of the crop usually took place in dikes or special ponds on the commons and the resulting linen was processed in people's homes or in small workshops or mills. At the beginning of the twentieth century, there was still a 'line' or linen mill at Crowle.

While you will still see fields of oilseed rape in the Levels, the vast majority of arable crops grown in the area today consist of cereals; mostly wheat and barley. Another important modern crop is sugar beet, which is sent to the processing plants at York on the Ouse and Newark on the Trent.

Potatoes were a very important crop on the fertile newly 'warped' lands around Thorne and on the Isle of Axholme. Wheat and potatoes were often rotated, and beans inserted when there was a fear of soil exhaustion.

The area once even had its own eating apple, known as the Sykehouse Russet from the village where it

Intensive vegetable cropping near the M62 Boothferry motorway bridge

Beetroot in a field near Wroot

originated, and described as "one of the most excellent dessert apples." Its yellowish flesh was described as "firm, crisp and juicy, with a rich, sugary and very high flavour." Two type trial trees are being nutured at the Brogdale Orchards in Faversham, Kent.

Until the 1970s, the Isle of Axholme was a major centre for market gardening, with field vegetables and salad crops, such as peas, celery, leeks, carrots and other root crops being grown on the narrow strip fields which had escaped Parliamentary enclosure in the Georgian period. But since then, the local industry has been hit by the growth of supermarkets and competition from larger producers and foreign imports, and by the attraction of subsidies for cereal crops, so that today, there are only a few producers. The production of turf has also emerged as a popular modern 'crop'.

These changes also meant that the ancient cultivation strips were amalgamated into larger units, with the result that the ancient and attractive field patterns have been disappearing under intensive arable farming. Most recently, a special Countryside Stewardship Scheme was launched by Defra to try to save this unique farming landscape by encouraging strip cultivation in the fields around the Isle of Axholme.

Only in the smaller, poorly-drained fields around Fishlake and Sykehouse are stock-raising of cattle and sheep and dairying really important farm products, although there has been a recent increase in farms stocking free-range pigs. Fifty years ago, most of the farmers in the Levels were categorised as part-time, and the average size of farms was only 136 acres/55ha, well below the national average. Today, however, the average size of farm holdings is very much larger and the area is one of the most professional and productive arable areas in the country.

The recent downturn in the agricultural industry has seen many local farmers take the marketing initiative themselves, and Farmers' Markets are now held regularly at places like Doncaster, and in Epworth Market Place on the third Thursday of each month. The sourcing of local food is being actively promoted by groups such as the Doncaster and North Lincolnshire Local Food Network.

A growing number of smaller specialist growers

Free range pigs on the Levels

Combine harvester at work near Adlingfleet

have also recently sprung up, such as Stonecrop Herbs of East Lound, near Haxey, where you might be surprised to see oranges, lemons and other citrus fruit, and olives being grown in North Lincolnshire. Many varieties of herbs are also grown here, and herbal remedies are also on offer.

The Doncaster and North Lincolnshire Local Food Network is a recent initiative designed to encourage the sales of local produce in the area and further afield.

It concentrates on locally-grown, usually organic crops, fresh from the fields.

All this is in addition to the annual Epworth Agricultural Show held in August, and the famous Festival of the Plough held in September at Epworth, which draws competitors from across the country to test their skills at ploughing with vintage tractors. There are also displays of steam ploughing and threshing. The Crowle Agricultural Show, another fine

The Festival of the Plough, Epworth: Shire horses ploughing

example of the once-common but now-so-rare local farming show, is held earlier on in May.

Hunting and wildfowling has been a local tradition on the Levels since the days of the royal preserve of Hatfield Chase. One of these ancient skills, introduced from Holland, was that of duck decoys. In essence, these were shallow pools constructed in the marsh, surrounded by woodland. From the pool one or more curved, tapering extensions known as a 'pipes' were made, and covered over with netting hung over hoops which stretched across the pipes.

The ducks – usually mallard, wigeon and teal – were attracted to the pool by the use of semi-tame decoy ducks (hence the name) and then left to settle down and feel unthreatened for a few days. They were then skilfully lured, sometimes by a man progressively dropping feed and sometimes by following a trained dog known as a 'piper', to go down into the narrowing

Ploughing, Isle of Axholme

A traction engine pulling a steam plough

pipe to be trapped at the end in a closed net. It was said that "…one man could lure them into a pipe or pipes attached to it, and take all the profit to himself in a quiet and methodical manner."

Reminders of several of these star-shaped decoy ponds can still be found in place-names on the moors, but the skill of constructing and using them is now lost, as is the skill of wildfowling. An observer writing as long ago as 1890 complained:

Probably no other art, sport, or handicraft which has been handed down from the earliest times has more rapidly decayed under the influence of nineteenth century civilisation than that of 'wildfowling.' The drainage of the fens, and the invention and improvement of fire-arms, have rung the death-knell of the duck decoys, and driven the hordes of wildfowl that used to swarm every winter in the low-lying eastern counties to more remote and congenial haunts…

Peat extraction, or 'graving', has been important in the area since medieval times, and originally took place only on the 'turbaries' on common land, where it was taken on a small scale by the commoners using their right of turbary for winter fuel. Parish turbaries still exist at Belton, Haxey and Epworth – the latter two now being Lincolnshire Wildlife Trust nature reserves. While no longer exploited for peat, sand or timber, these areas – like the Crowle, Thorne and Hatfield Moors – represent precious survivals of the once-extensive common moors which extended across the Levels.

Commercial peat extraction began in the 1880s when the Thorne Moors Improvement Company, which had taken over much of the common land, began to drain and cut large areas. It continued by hand-cutting and transporting by horse-drawn wagons until Fisons acquired the British Moss Litter Company, the successor to the Thorne Moors Improvement Company, in 1963 and introduced machine-milling on an industrial scale. Large-scale commercial peat extraction is now gradually being brought to a close, and the peat workings are being restored for their wildlife and nature conservation interest, with its associated benefits for the economy and tourism of the area.

An important, often unrealised, product of the Humberhead Levels has been energy. First came the small-scale extraction of peat for local use as fuel; then the once-great coal mining industry, which started in the Conisbrough area in the late nineteenth century and later spread east in the South Yorkshire coalfield; and finally the huge coal-fed power stations in the Trent and Aire Valleys.

Today, more sustainable and lower carbon alternatives are being explored in the area, such as the Project Arbre wood-fuelled power station at Eggborough, which uses short-rotation coppice willow for fuel. New crops are also being used to create biofuels as the search goes on for more sustainably-produced energy.

10. Getting There

Despite its apparant isolation, the Humberhead Levels are surprisingly easy to get to, whether you come by land, sea or air, and there is a good rail and bus public transport network when you arrive.

By road

Most people will arrive by road, and the Humberhead Levels finds itself at the heart of a speedy motorway network which comprises the A1(M) running north-south past Doncaster to the east; the M18 running from Sheffield to the M62 (use junctions 4, 5 or 6); the M62 running east-west north of Goole (junctions 35, 36, 37 or 38), and the M180 which joins the M18 at Junction 5 near Thorne, from Grimsby and Scunthorpe (junctions 1, 2 or 3).

The M180 cuts across the Levels

The M18 Ouse Bridge

The area is about 20 minutes from York, 30 minutes from Hull or Lincoln, 45 minutes from Sheffield and an hour from Leeds. There is also a very good A trunk road system, including the north-south, A19 Doncaster-Selby; A614 Bawtry-Goole, and A161 Beckingham-Goole roads, and the east-west A63 Leeds-Selby-Hull road.

By rail

The East Coast Main Line runs through Doncaster from London Kings Cross, and there are local connections to Stainforth, Thorne and Goole. There are also links to Barnetby, Scunthorpe, and Crowle. The Leeds-Hull line has stops at Selby, Wressle, Eastrington, Staddlethorpe, and Brough.

A direct rail link operates from Scunthorpe to

A train pulls out of Thorne station

Manchester Airport, which is less than two hours away. Enquiries 08457 484950.

By Bus

There are many local and express bus services serving villages throughout the area.

For more information, contact 01757 703263 (Selby TIC); 01302 734309 (Doncaster TIC), or 01652 657053 (Brigg TIC).

By sea

The P&O North Sea Ferries terminal at Hull is about 45 minutes drive away from the Humberhead Levels area. It provides daily sailings to Zeebrugge and Rotterdam. Enquiries on 08701 296002.

By air

The Humberside International Airport is situated on the A18 between Brigg and Grimsby, not far from the M180. As already stated, there is a direct rail link between Scunthorpe and Manchester Airport, which is less than two hours away, while the East Midlands Airport at Castle Donington is about the same distance, linked by the M18 to the M1.

The recent £80 million development of the former RAF airbase at Finningley as the 'Robin Hood Doncaster Sheffield' international airport within the Levels will obviously provide another key gateway to the Humberhead area.

11. What to Do

The distinctive silhouette of a nightjar in flight waymarks the route of the Peatlands Way, a 45-mile circular long-distance footpath which will take you through the heart of the Humberhead Levels. In this chapter, we will follow it to get a taste of the walking opportunities of the area and its varied landscape and history.

The Peatlands Way visits the historic setttlements of Thorne, Crowle, Belton, Epworth, Haxey, Wroot, and Kirk Bramwith, as it makes its great loop around the Levels. It includes the first permissive paths to cross the internationally-important nature reserves of Thorne and Hatfield Moors, which had been barred to walkers for many years.

Peatlands Way waymark

The Way has been broken up into four sections: Thorne to Crowle, Crowle to Epworth, Epworth to Wroot and Wroot to Stainforth to enable day walks to be undertaken based on circular routes linked by public transport on the four sections.

The initiative of the Humberhead Levels Green Tourism Forum, the Peatlands Way also links with the 215-mile coast-to-coast Trans-Pennine Trail between Liverpool and Hull at Bramwith and Sykehouse on the

Walkers on the former Axholme railway line at Belton

Trans-Pennine Trail sign

Cyclists enjoying traffic-free riding on the Axholme Line at Belton

New Junction Canal, the Isle of Axholme Greenway and the Thorne Round Walk.

Most people start the Peatlands Way at the Delves Fishponds west of Thorne, where there is a convenient public transport link as they are opposite Thorne North railway station, near Capitol Park, and there is also a café. The walk heads north parallel to the roar of the M18 motorway towards Moorends, which is skirted to the south.

Crossing Thorne Moors to the east can be dangerous and it is advisable to keep to the paths as the old peat workings and drainage ditches contain deep water and the ankle-sucking peat itself can be treacherous. You might be lucky enough to spot merlin, sparrowhawk or hen harrier as you cross the moors, and on a summer's evening, you may even hear the spinechilling 'churring' call of the elusive nightjar.

Crowle is the next stop on the route and the path crosses The Warpings (see Chapter 8) and Crowle Moors, and equally rich in rare flora and fauna. Then after passing Tetley Ponds, where there are watersport facilities, the first 10 miles are completed when you reach Crowle Station, by Crowle Wharf on the Stainforth and Keadby Canal. This is another useful public transport link.

The route now heads south crossing the Double

Rivers of the North Engine Drain and the Hatfield Waste Drain before passing under the M180, then following the Temple Drain. This area was once wild marshland and peatbog, but was first drained by Vermuyden and his Dutch engineers in the seventeenth century when the three main rivers of the Idle, the Don and the Torne were diverted.

We are now heading directly towards the higher ground of the Isle of Axholme, once truly an island in the surrounding marshes and peat bogs. We enter the village of Belton – the amalgamation of eight small hamlets, including Church Town where the parish church of All Saints is situated – via Stealgoose Lane. Nearby is the estate of Temple Belwood, which has connections with the Knights Templar of Balsall.

In another three miles we reach Epworth, the capital of Axholme and the largest settlement on the 'island.' A visit to the Heritage Centre in the centre of the town

Angler on the Stainforth and Keadby Canal

is recommended for an explanation of the unique medieval strip farming systems which still exist in this area, and in few other places in Britain. Epworth is also, of course, the birthplace of world Methodism and the former home of John Wesley, who is commemorated in the Old Rectory Museum and the Wesley Memorial Church.

Heading south again, it is three miles and a half miles across the fields to Haxey, the home of the famous Haxey Hood Game, described as 'Britain's oldest tussle', which takes place through the streets and fields of Haxey and Westwoodside every January.

We follow the significantly-named Turbary Road (the ancient right of turbary was to cut turfs, or peat blocks, from the moor for fuel) west from Haxey towards the now-wooded local nature reserve of Haxey Turbary. Heading north now, the Way goes along the Greenholme Bank and Greenholme Lane Drain for a mile, before turning west (left) passing the Tunnel Pits Bridge and Pumping Station.

This was the former junction of the Rivers Torne and Idle, and the raised artificial cut of the River Torne here was originally engineered by Vermuyden, the lower course being the soak dyke. The red brick pumping station at Tunnel Pits was built in 1962 to take low-level water from the north and south into the Torne.

The linear village of Wroot is the next stop, two miles away across the flat fields and drains, with their enormous skies. Wroot is thought to get its unusual name from the Old English for a 'snout', and it is thought that the raised spur of land on which it stands must have resembled a pig's snout.

We turn north at Wroot and then west again to enter the National Nature Reserve of Hatfield Moors, much of which has been decimated by commercial peat diggings, but there are extensive areas of birch and oak woodland, and large, tranquil pools created by the extraction of sand and gravel over the years.

After turning north and passing by many of these attractive pools and the fences of H.M. Hatfield Prison, the Way heads for the village of Hatfield Woodhouse, which takes its name from the fact that it was formerly the site of a hunting lodge for the kings and noblemen who once hunted on Hatfield Chase.

Passing under the M18 again, the Way now heads west between Stainforth and Fishlake, which is famous for its medieval field systems and its thirteenth century parish church, unusually dedicated to St Cuthbert.

The Way joins the Trans-Pennine Trail again after two and a half miles at Kirk Bramwith, where the parish church of St Mary has magnificent stained glass, and furnishings by 'Mouseman' – Robert Thompson of Kilburn.

Another footpath route which traverses the western part of the Levels is the 70-mile Danum Way, which was inaugurated by the Doncaster Group of the Ramblers' Association to mark its Diamond Jubilee in 1996. The sections between Askern, Sykehouse,

Birdwatching at Duffield Carrs

Fishlake, Stainforth, Hatfield and Lindholme cross the area of the Humberhead Levels, and there is an excellent guidebook covering the route by David Ward.

An easier although linear walk is the 12-mile

Viewing platform, Thorne Moors

Axholme Line, which follows the course of the disused railway between Crowle, Belton, Epworth and Haxey north-south along the length of the Isle of Axholme, and is perfect for families, cyclists or horseriders. Shorter routes include the Wesley Trail around Epworth and the series of leaflets produced by the Town Council which describe walks around Thorne. In the north of the area, the 9½ mile Pocklington Canal towpath between East Cottingwith on the Derwent and Canal Head, near Pocklington on the foothills of the Yorkshire Wolds, is very popular with walkers and anglers.

The maze of green lanes, minor roads and canal towpaths which criss-cross the Levels are perfect for walkers, cyclists and horseriders wanting a traffic-free experience, and the numerous lakes such as the Seven Lakes Leisure Park at Ealand, near Crowle, provide a variety of watersports. Fishing is available under licence on many of the lakes and drains.

Birdwatchers are spoilt for choice in the area of the Humberhead Levels. With so many national and local nature reserves, many of which provide convenient hides, there is a wealth of opportunities for twitchers. Perhaps the best opportunities for observing rarities will be found in English Nature's Humberhead Peatlands National Nature Reserves where species such as the nightjar, hobby, marsh harrier and nightingale (at its northernmost outpost in Britain here) can be seen or heard. There is a large viewing platform close to the Cottage Dyke to the east of Moorends, near Thorne.

The over-wintering populations of swans, geese, ducks and waders in the Lower Derwent Valley National Nature Reserve are vast and make these wetlands of international importance. During the spring and summer, the flower-filled meadows are alive with nesting wildfowl and waders, such as lapwings, redshank, curlew, snipe and teal, wigeon and shoveler.

Hides are provided at Bank Island and Wheldrake Ings, to the north of the site, and at North Duffield Carrs in the south, where there is also access for wheelchair users.

Moored narrow boats on the Stainforth and Keadby Canal

12. Where to Go

Modern visitors to the Humberhead Levels are following in the footsteps of royalty. The region has been a popular destination of kings and princes ever since, according to local tradition, Henry I, the youngest son of William the Conquerer, was born in **Selby**, and medieval kings and princes used the marshy wastes of Thorne Mere on **Hatfield Chase** for hunting.

Brodsworth Hall from the croquet lawn

Normanby Hall

Thorne Mere may have disappeared, but the royal connections with the foundations of **Selby Abbey** are well-established. Henry I (1100-35) issued an order that the abbey of St Germaine at Selby, founded by his father and mother, Queen Matilda, should not be moved. So when Abbot Hugh rebuilt the stately abbey in the early years of the twelfth century in the Norman and Early Gothic styles, he had to stay on the sandy site close to the River Ouse, which is just three feet above the water table. This had been the cause of much damaging settlement over the years, and the collapse of the central tower in 1690. The Abbey, continuing as one of the most magnificent parish churches in England, survived not only the Dissolution of the Monasteries in the sixteenth century, but also a great fire in 1906. The wonderful alternating designs of the Norman arches of the chancel bear a great resemblance to those in Durham Cathedral.

Another fine church, although one which suffered badly at the hands of Henry VIII's troops at the Dissolution, is **Howden Minster**. Although partly now in ruins, it retains its magnificent fourteenth century Perpendicular crossing tower, which rivals Boston's famous 'Stump.' Inside is the Saltmarshe chantry, which contains a number of fine medieval effigies including a knight in chain mail, and a rare stone pulpitum with a wooden altar by 'Mouseman' Robert Thompson of Kilburn. Nearby in the bustling port of Goole is the **Goole Waterways Museum**, which traces the history of the port and the network of waterways which thread the area.

Epworth is the natural centre for the exploration of the Isle of Axholme, and a place of pilgrimage for Methodists from all over the world. **The Old Rectory** was the Wesley family home until 1735. The present Queen Anne building replaced the original thatched Rectory after a fire in 1709, from which the five-year-old John Wesley was rescued, as his mother said: "a brand plucked from the burning". Today it is a museum with rooms furnished and laid out as the Wesleys would have known it.

At the other end of the High Street is the **Wesley Memorial Chapel** erected in 1889 to the memory of Charles and John Wesley, the founders of world

The Waterways Museum, Goole

Methodism. The striking chancel window shows the two brothers above a depiction of the risen Christ. The **Epworth Heritage Centre** is housed in the Market Court House, the oldest secular building in Epworth, and it displays a comprehensive archive of the village's past, including the seventeenth century drainage of the surrounding area.

St Andrew's Parish Church at Epworth is where Samuel Wesley, John's father, was rector, and where both John and Charles were baptised and worshipped as children. Samuel's tomb lies outside the south door, and this was where John, having been barred from preaching inside the church because of his radical beliefs, memorably preached one of his stirring sermons in 1742.

Some smaller **village churches** which are nevertheless interesting and always well worth a visit include St Cuthbert's at Fishlake, St Oswald's at Crowle, St Nicholas at Thorne, St Lawrence at Hatfield, and on the edge of the area, St Peter's at Conisbrough and St Mary's at Tickhill.

Sandtoft lies close to the M180 two miles to the north west of Epworth, and is the home of two major visitor attractions in the **Sandtoft Transport Museum** and **Imperial Aviation**. The Transport Museum is the home to Britain's largest collection of preserved trolleybuses and buses. You can take a ride on a 1930s trolleybus and enjoy the 1950s shop displays and film shows. Special 'Trolley Days' are held from Easter to October.

You can learn to fly and see the Levels from the air by visiting **Imperial Aviation** at Sandtoft, where comprehensive flight training or half-hour introductory flying lessons can be arranged. Restoration is underway on the site on a number of vintage aircraft, including Avro Lancaster and Lincoln bombers, an

Gloster Meteor, Imperial Aviation, Sandtoft

American Mitchell B-25 bomber, and early De Havilland Vampire jet fighters.

Once every village had its own blacksmith, and you can relive those days by a visit to the **Owston Ferry Smithy and Heritage Centre**. Owston Ferry is on the River Trent about two miles south east of Epworth, and as the name suggests, marks the site of an ancient ferry across the river. The Heritage Centre and Smithy in the High Street shows a Victorian smithy as it looked about a century ago. There is an exhibition of old farming tools in the courtyard, with a fascinating village museum on the first floor.

Another museum which shows country life as it was is the North Lincolnshire Farming Museum at the 300-acre/121ha **Normanby Hall Country Park**, four miles north of Scunthorpe. The museum is based on the refined Regency building of Normanby Hall, designed by Robert Smirke, with its Victorian walled garden. The hall and museum is open from Easter until September.

Another stately home worth a visit is **Carlton Towers** six miles south of Selby on the A1041. The rather severe stucco-clad mock-Gothic exterior was designed by J.F.Bentley, the designer of Westminster Cathedral, and it masks a seventeenth century manor house complete with a priest's hole upstairs. **Brodsworth Hall and Gardens**, (English Heritage) near Doncaster, is an Italianate mansion dating from the 1860s, and is one of the country's most complete surviving Victorian country houses. The gardens also preserve the 1860 design and include the romantic quarry garden with its fashionable fern dell.

Recently benefiting from a £4 million Heritage Lottery Grant for its renovation, **Cusworth Hall** on a limestone ridge in the northern suburbs of Doncaster, commands a panoramic view across the town. It was built in 1741 for the Wrightson family, and 10 years later, the pedimented wings, containing the chapel and billiard rooms, were added by Joseph Paine. It is now run as a museum of rural life by Doncaster Borough Council, and the parklands and lakes are also open to the public.

Hatfield Water Park

Blacktoft Sands RSPB Reserve

Also in South Yorkshire but well worth a visit are the splendid remains of **Conisbrough Castle**, on the A630 between Doncaster and Rotherham, the principal stronghold of the de Warenne family, Earls of Surrey since the eleventh century (English Heritage). The dominating cylindrical keep is reckoned to be one of the finest in England, and has recently been re-roofed and re-floored, and there is an excellent visitor centre and restaurant.

Nearby at Templeborough is the award-winning **Magna Science Adventure Centre**, constructed within the old Templeborough Steel Works. Here children of all ages can experience the thrills of the new Power Pavilion, the awesome Earth and Fire Pavilions, and the drenching Water Pavilion. It's a hands-on, no-holds-barred scientific experience that will take your breath away. Definitely not for the faint-hearted!

If wildlife watching is your thing, then there are visitor facilities and hides at places like the Yorkshire Wildlife Trust's **Potteric Carr** reserve near Doncaster; at places like **Bank Island, Wheldrake Ings** and **North Duffield Carrs** on the Lower Derwent Valley National Nature Reserve on the River Derwent; on the RSPB's reserve at **Blacktoft Sands**, near Ousefleet, and the **Humberhead Peatlands National Nature Reserve.**

13. Gazetteer of Towns and Villages

Askern

Unlikely as it may seem, during the nineteenth century Askern was a spa town which rivalled Harrogate and Scarborough. The source of its fame was a well which was discovered to contain sulphate of magnesia, and a spa developed from around 1814 to accommodate the influx of people coming for the cure. It is believed that the Romans knew of the health-giving properties of the well, because the legend is that there are Roman remains beneath the calm waters of Askern Lake in the centre of the former coal-mining village. At Sutton Common on the southern outskirts of Askern, an important Iron Age 'marsh-fort' has recently been excavated.

Austerfield village sign

Austerfield

William Bradford, one of the original Pilgrim Fathers who crossed the Atlantic to America in the *Mayflower* in 1620, is traditionally thought to have been born at Austerfield Manor, the son of a yeoman farmer, in 1589/90. He became involved with the Separatist Church at nearby Scrooby and fled to Holland in 1607, returning to England to join the *Mayflower* pilgrims. Bradford went on to become the long-serving Governor and historian of Plymouth County in what is now Massachusetts, New England. There is a statue to him on the Plymouth, Massachusetts, Waterfront.

Barnby Dun

Five miles north east of Doncaster and in the heart of the former South Yorkshire coalfield, Barnby Dun takes its name from the River Don. The parish church of St Peter and Paul has a fine Perpendicular tower and both the large chancel and beautiful north aisle date from the fourteenth century. There are also some fine nineteenth century furnishings and a monument by Scheemakers in the interior.

Bawtry

Bawtry is a neat little planned town laid out at the end of the twelfth century to take advantage of the trade brought via the River Idle and the towns of Rotherham and Sheffield to the west. It later thrived because of its proximity to the junction of the Great North Road turnpike. It was once a vitally important port for the export of millstones quarried in the Peak District, as well as knives and blades from Sheffield. Some of the more prominent buildings include the medieval parish church of St Nicholas, the late seventeenth century gabled Dutch House in Church Street, and The Crown, a former coaching inn, in the mainly Georgian High Street.

Belton

Belton is on the A161 and was created by the amalgamation of no less than eight hamlets. It lies at the centre of one of the best remaining examples of medieval strip fields, created from the open field system. It was a wealthy area in Norman times, but the only remaining Norman work is the circular font in the north aisle at All Saints Church. There is now just one Methodist chapel where there were once four, and only two surviving shops. The area of Temple Gardens to the east of the village was once owned by the Knights Templar.

Church Fenton

The name of Church Fenton has evolved over the years, starting as *Fentune* in 963 to *Fentun* in the Doomsday Book. Kirk Fenton is first mentioned 1338 signifying the establishment of a church in the village. It is likely that the origins of the village were agricultural, although in 1400 records show that many villagers were employed at the Huddleston stone quarry at a time when the stone was being used to build York Cathedral. The Perpendicular parish church of St Mary is said to be one of the smallest cruciform churches in the country. It was built using stone from the Huddleston quarry. The original vicarage is the present 'Old Vicarage' opposite the Methodist Chapel, which dates from at least 1663. The present Methodist Chapel built in 1892 was preceded by an earlier chapel built in 1804 and probably attached at some point to Wesley House.

The RAF training station at Church Fenton (which is actually in the neighbouring village of Norse-sounding Ulleskelf) was built in 1937 and was used as a fighter base for Spitfires and Hurricanes during the Battle of Britain in 1940.

Crowle

Crowle, a former market town, lies to the north of the Isle of Axholme. St Oswald's Church dates back to the twelfth century and contains the Crowle Stone – a rare Anglo-Scandinavian carved cross shaft which probably dates to the ninth or tenth centuries. It was formerly reused by Norman masons as a lintel over the west door, but was rescued and restored in 1919, when its age and importance were recognised. Much of the town centre – bisected by a busy one-way system – is now a conservation area, containing many fine Georgian and Victorian buildings set around the attractive old market square.

Doncaster

Founded by the Romans as *Danum*, the borough of Doncaster is a delightful blend of urban and rural charm where the vibrant town centre is complemented by historic villages and market towns. Doncaster's Mansion House, one of only three in England, is a fine example of Georgian architecture. Dominating the town's skyline is the stately tower of St George's Church, a masterpiece by George Gilbert Scott, architect of St Pancras Station. There is some fine Victorian stained glass, especially the east window. Doncaster Market has a charter which dates from 1248, and features over 600 stalls. Additionally,

Frenchgate Centre boasts High Street stores and designer boutiques and Lakeside Village, just two miles from the town centre offers outlet shopping. Nearby are the stately homes of Brodsworth and Cusworth Halls.

One of the town's most famous attractions is Doncaster Racecourse where the highlight of the annual racing calendar is the historic four-day St Leger Festival. This is the oldest of the racing calendar's classics and has been held every September since 1776.

Epworth

Epworth, birthplace of world Methodism, is also the 'capital' of the Isle of Axholme. With a unique mixture of Wesleyan heritage, speciality shopping and traditional inns and tea-rooms, Epworth is a fascinating place to visit.

You can trace the history of the founder of Methodism, John Wesley, by following the Wesley Trail. This visits places like the Georgian red brick Old Rectory where John Wesley grew up, St Andrew's Church where his father Samuel was Rector, and the Wesley Methodist Memorial Church, dedicated to the memory of both John and his brother Charles Wesley. A fine statue of John Wesley stands on Albion Hill close to the Old Rectory.

Outside the church is the tomb of Samuel Wesley, where John once preached having been banned from the church. Another of Wesley's outdoor pulpits was Epworth's ancient market cross.

You can discover Epworth's chilling past by taking one of the popular Ghost Walks which run through the winter months, learning about Old Jeffrey, one of the best-documented poltergeists in the country, who haunted the Wesley family.

Fishlake

The magnificent thirteenth century St Cuthbert's Parish Church at Fishlake reflects the former prosperity of the village, which was once an inland port on the River Don. Originally built by the Normans, the church is reputed to be a resting place of the body of the saint on its way to burial at Durham. His remains were carried by his faithful monks for seven years

The silhouette of the needle-like spire of Hemingbrough church

from about 875 AD over a wide area between the Humber and the Tweed, in order to escape the attention of Viking invaders. It was not until 300 years after his death that St Cuthbert's earthly remains reached their final resting place in 995 in Durham Cathedral. The network of small, hedged fields which are closest to the village date back to medieval times, contrasting strongly with the Enclosure Act 'prairie' landscape beyond.

Goole

Of Britain's sea ports, Goole is one of the furthest inland, situated where the Don meets the Ouse, over 40 miles from the North Sea, which is reached via the Humber Estuary. The rapid growth of Goole as a port is relatively recent, dating from 1826, when the docks were built and the Aire and Calder Navigation was built from Knottingley. The main cargo used to be coal from the adjacent South Yorkshire coalfield, but today almost everything is carried in containers, especially large numbers of imported cars and timber.

Haxey

Haxey, just off the A161, is famed for its historic game of the Haxey Hood. Legend has it that 600 years ago Lady de Mowbray lost her hood in a gust of wind, sending farmworkers chasing after it. Every year since then pub-goers re-enact the scene by scrambling to retrieve a symbolic hood. Haxey is also home to the disused Axholme railway line, parts of which are open to the public.

Hemingbrough

Overshadowed by the huge cooling towers of the Drax power station, the slender spire of St Mary's Church, Hemingbrough, rises 180 feet/55m above the flat countryside. Since it was built before the Norman Conquest, St Mary's has been added to by successive generations, and contains some particularly fine medieval woodwork.

Howden

Formerly the site of the biggest horse fair in England, Howden is a former market town which was once owned by the Bishops of Durham and gave its name to the surrounding district, which was known as 'Howdenshire.' The Minster church of St Peter and Paul is actually the west end of the former collegiate church, the picturesque ruins of the rest of which are now set in a garden. The magnificent Decorated west front is its chief glory, along with the pulpitum or stone screen which once divided the collegiate east end of the church from the parochial west. The medieval Saltmarshe tombs in the chancel have a significant name.

Misterton

The name of this small village at the southern end of the Isle of Axholme may come from the Saxon 'Ministreton', or the village or town attached to a monastery or church.

Newport

Newport, near the northern terminus of the M62, used to boast one of the earliest Methodist chapels in the old East Riding of Yorkshire, over a ground floor which consisted of shops and houses. Newport did not exist before 1780, but following the drainage of Wallingfen, which was aided by the construction of the Market Weighton Canal, good quality clays were discovered, which resulted in the development of brickworks and the creation of the village.

Owston Ferry

Owston Ferry, as the name suggests, marks a former ferry point across the River Trent, two miles east of Epworth and the Isle of Axholme. It is a pleasant backwater of a village, grouped around its market square. To the west of the village behind the church are the remains of a Norman motte and bailey castle, later refortified and known as Kinnaird Castle and the home of the Mowbray family. In the High Street is the red brick Owston Ferry Smithy and Heritage Centre, which shows the village smithy as it looked a century ago. There is an exhibition of old farming tools in the courtyard, and the village museum is on the first floor.

Retford

This mainly Victorian north Nottinghamshire coal mining town is in two parts, separated by the River Idle and linked by the town bridge. The chiefly fifteenth century parish church of St Swithun suffered a catastrophic collapse of its central tower in 1651, but it was imaginatively rebuilt on the remaining four thirteenth century arches.

Seaton Ross

Seaton Ross is an isolated village in the far north of the area, which used to boast two windmills and is perhaps best known now for the pantiled cottage on the main street with an outsize sundial, framing an upstairs window, on its front. This was reputedly the work of William Watson, a nineteenth century farmer and surveyor who had a similar sundial on the front of his nearby farmhouse, and a smaller one on the village church.

Sandtoft

The Trolleybus Museum at Sandtoft, near Epworth, is home to Britain's largest collection of preserved trolleybuses. Regular 'Trolleydays' are held from Easter to October and the annual Sandtoft Gathering sees motorbuses arriving from all over the country.

Selby

Selby is an unspoilt market town with traditional community values, romantic history and lovely countryside – all easily accessible as it lies between the M62 and A1/M1. Walkers and cyclists love the surrounding landscape, especially the Transpennine Trail cycle way with its direct link into the heart of York.

Selby Abbey – often described as one of the most magnificent parish churches in England – was founded in AD1069 by the monk Benedict following approval by William the Conqueror. William's fourth son was born at Selby, and went on to become King Henry I. The nave is mainly Norman and has a bay system and massive round pillars like those in Durham Cathedral. The beautiful choir is in the Decorated style and features the fourteenth century Washington window containing the family coat of arms – thought by many

Sundial cottage, Seaton Ross

to be the forerunner of the present day US Stars and Stripes flag.

Sherburn in Elmet

Sherburn's days as a flying town date back to the First World War, where a field to the east of the town was used by the Royal Flying Corps. At the start of the Second World War, Sherburn was taken over by RAF Fighter Command and was used by Church Fenton as a satellite airfield. The fighters eventually left the airfield in 1941, and because of ideal transportation facilities and access, the site was developed for aircraft production by Blackburn Aircraft Ltd. With the end of the war, the airfield returned to its civilian status and today, only a small part of the site is used for flying by the Sherburn Aero Club.

Stainforth

The name means 'stone ford' and it marks an ancient crossing of the River Don. Stainforth was one of the last places in the country to receive a market charter, granted by Edward III in 1348, and its market square remains. One of Stainforth's greatest advantages was that it served the villages of Thorne and the Isle of Axholme whose wares were landed here, before hiring horses to complete the journey to Doncaster market. The Stainforth-Keadby Canal opened in 1797, and linked with the River Trent via the Don.

Sykehouse

Sykehouse – the Old English name means 'the house on the stream' – is said to be the longest village in Yorkshire, stretching for nearly eight miles along the long main street. It is surrounded by ancient field systems, and although many of the hedges may have been planted after the local Enclosure Award of 1825, some may date back to medieval or Tudor times. A locally common species is the white willow, and Sykehouse also once boasted its own dessert apple, the Sykehouse Russet.

Thorne

The parish church of St Nicholas is mainly Early English in style, and it boasts a fine Decorated tower which overlooks the former mining village. Beside the church to the north in the park are the remains of a Norman motte and bailey castle. Close by are the extensive peat workings of Thorne Moors, and at Moorends, part of the Humberhead Peatlands National Nature Reserve.

Wroot

In a desolate part of the Isle of Axholme, with the expanse of Hatfield Moors to the north, Wroot's skyline is broken only by rows of planted poplars and the red brick tower of the parish church. John Wesley was curate at St Pancras between 1727 and 1729, when his father Samuel was rector of Wroot and Epworth. The present church dates from a major reconstruction in 1879. Wroot is famous for its crops of red beetroot and potatoes.

14. Useful Addresses

The Countryside Agency
Yorkshire & The Humber Region
4th Floor, Victoria Wharf
No 4, The Embankment
Sovereign Street
Leeds LS1 4BA
Tel: 0113 246 9222

Doncaster Museum & Art Gallery
Chequer Road
Doncaster
DN1 2AE
Tel: 01302 734289

English Nature
Humber and Pennines Team
Bullring House
Northgate
Wakefield
West Yorkshire WF1 3BJ
Tel: 01924 387010

English Nature
North and East Yorkshire Team
Genesis 1
University Road
Heslington
York YO10 5ZQ
Tel: 01904 435500

Epworth Tourism Partnership
North Lincolnshire District Council
Church Square House
PO Box 42
Scunthorpe
North Lincs DN15 6QX
Tel: 01724 297356

Lincolnshire Trust for Nature Conservation
Banovallum House
Manor House Street
Horncastle
Lincolnshire LN9 5HF
Tel: 01507 526667

RSPB N.W. England
Westleigh Mews
Wakefield Road
Denby Dale
Huddersfield HD8 8QD
Tel: 01484 861148

Thorne-Moorends Town Council
Assembly Rooms
Fieldside
Thorne
South Yorkshire DN8 4AE
Tel: 01405 812092

Yorkshire Tourist Board
312 Tadcaster Road
York
YO24 1GS
Tel: 01904 773321

Yorkshire Wildlife Trust
10 Toft Green
York YO1 6JT
Tel: 01904 659570

Further Reading

Anon – *Countryside Character Vol. 3: Yorkshire & The Humber* (1998), Countryside Commission

Anon (poss. John Harrison) – *The Manuscript in a Red Box* (1903, reprinted 1974), Doncaster Free Press

Broadhead, Ivan E. – *Portrait of Humberside* (1983), Robert Hale

Broadhead, Ivan E. – *Portrait of the Yorkshire Ouse* (1982), Robert Hale

Caufield, Catherine; photographs by Godwin, Fay – *Thorne Moors* (1991), Sumach Press

Cory, Vernon – *Hatfield and Axholme – An Historical Review* (1985), Providence Press

Duckham, Baron F. – *The Yorkshire Ouse* (1967), David & Charles

Fairclough, Graham ed. – *Historic Landscape Characterisation* (1999), English Heritage.

Hattersley, Roy – *A Brand from the Burning – The Life of John Wesley* (2002), Little, Brown

John K. Johnstone – *The Isle of Axholme; its place-names and river-names* (1886, reprinted 1983), Smith Settle

Miller, Keith – *The Isle of Axholme Historic Landscape Characterisation Project* (1997), Countryside Commission

Purseglove, Jeremy – *Taming the Flood* (1988), Oxford University Press

Rollins, Julian – *Land Marks* (2003), English Nature

Smith, Roly ed. – *The Marsh of Time –Saving Sutton Common* (2004) Halsgrove

Taylor, Martin – *Thorne Mere & The Old River Don* (1987), William Sessions

Van de Noort, Robert – *The Humber Wetlands – The Archaeology of a Dynamic Landscape* (2004), Windgather Press

Various – *Thorne & Hatfield Moors Papers* (1997-2003), Thorne & Hatfield Moors Conservation Forum

Ward, David C – *The Danum Trail* (1996), The Ramblers' Association

Wright, Geoffrey – *Yorkshire:The East Riding* (1976), B.T.Batsford

Maps

The recommended maps for the detailed exploration on foot of the area are the four 2½ in to the mile, 1:25,000 Ordnance Survey Explorer sheets Nos. 279, Doncaster, Conisbrough, Maltby and Thorne; 280, Isle of Axholme, Scunthorpe and Gainsborough; 290, York, Selby and Tadcaster, and 291, Goole & Gilberdyke, Holme-on-Spaulding-Moor, Hemingbrough & Howden.

The larger scale 1½ in to the mile 1:50,000 Landranger sheets Nos 105, York and Selby; 106, Market Weighton; 111, Sheffield and Doncaster, and 112, Scunthorpe and Gainsborough, also cover the area and are useful for car-borne exploration.